AF540714

HOSPITALITY FAIRS AND EVENT

HOSPITALITY FAIRS AND EVENT

By
Nancy Brown

DISCOVERY PUBLISHING HOUSE PVT. LTD.
NEW DELHI-110 002

Published by:
Namit Wasan
DISCOVERY PUBLISHING HOUSE PVT. LTD.
4383/4B, Ansari Road, Darya Ganj
New Delhi-110 002 (India)
Phone : +91-11-23279245; 23253475; 43596065
E-mail : discoverybooksindia@gmail.com
discoverypublishinghouse@gmail.com
namitwasan9@gmail.com
web : www.discoverypublishinggroup.com

First Published: **2011**

Reprinted: **2021**

ISBN: 978-81-8356-923-1

Hospitality Fairs and Event

Printed at:
Infinity Imaging Systems
Delhi

PREFACE

The hospitality Industry becomes the hub of business activity for hotel business and hospitality industry which gives potential and current market players of hotels construction and hotel arrangements branch an opportunity to familiarize with a complex of offers on establishment of hotels with a turn-key solution.

Hospitality Fair and Event is an annual function that occurs in almost all parts of globe throughout the year. But the Restaurant Show London 2010 steal the limelight. It took place at Earls Court 2 from 11th to 13th October. Global visitors to this year's restaurant show feasted their eyes, ears, and taste buds on the new and exciting products available to shake up their offering.

If anyone can work for, with or in an independent restaurant, a restaurant chain, a gastro pub, a contract caterer, a bar or a hotel group, then one cannot afford to miss The Restaurant Show 2010. The Restaurant Show was more than an exhibition - it's a day out. The visitors saw over 350 major suppliers, source new products, visit our inspirational features and see talks and demonstrations.

The Workshop organized by Visit USA in cooperation with Commercial Service is held annually. It is known to be the best event for US travel professionals in Belgium. It gives a golden opportunity to promote USA tourism regions, products and services to the Belgium and Luxembourg markets. The workshop is exclusively open to travel agents and press. The 2008 Workshop showcased 45 exhibiting organizations and was attended by over 200 travel agents and fifteen travel journalists. Both exhibitors and visitors commented on the 2008 Workshop.

The Florida Restaurant & Lodging Show is a complete learning experience that improves one's business throughout. From new products, to new tricks of the trade, to gold-standard food service education, one will gain real-world solutions one can apply to their business immediately.

Dubai is the centre of attraction for any visitors. The Hotel Show 2011 will take place at the Dubai World Trade Centre from 17th – 19th May 2011 for its 12th edition. The show is renowned for its world class display of products, designs and technologies and will showcase the full spectrum of the hospitality industry. In 2010, The Hotel Show welcomed 365 exhibitors from 35 countries and attracted 10,277 key industry decision makers from 78 countries worldwide. Join The Hotel Show 2011 and access a market valued at over US $30bn with an ongoing projects pipeline of over 450 hotels and 1,500 F&B outlets across the GCC, Middle East & Levant markets.

The Tourism Business Council of South Africa is the official umbrella organisation for the travel and tourism private sector in South Africa. As a corporate association, the TBCSA strives to work together with all role players to create an enabling environment for growth and development of the tourism industry. The TBCSA originated the HICA concept in 2007 and is the primary driver behind this annual industry event for Southern Africa.

—Author

CONTENTS

1

INTRODUCTION

Hospitality is treating people like you would want to be treated when you are travelling. In other words, it means making a tourist feel totally welcome as not only your guest, but also the guest of the complete family of the Hotel. Hospitality is genuine smiling face.

Hospitality can be termed as deliberate, planned and sustained effort to establish and maintain mutual understanding between an organization and public i.e. business of making and keeping friends, and promoting an atmosphere of better understanding.

Very frequently we hear phrases like "He is always hospitable to visitors", "We are grateful to friends for their hospitality in putting us up while we were on holiday", "She is so inhospitable that she grudges giving us any thing to eat or drink when we visit her" etc. All such statements are suggesting the positive or negative attitude of welcome towards visitors, friends or strangers. Hospitality activity covers everything i.e. providing attentive and courteous services, facilities and amenities to a traveller, meeting and greeting him at the door, providing efficient and caring service of food and beverage to him in the room i.e. providing "A Home away from Home", and making his visit a memorable and pleasant experience.

Reception, welcome and, in general, the treatment of a guest or a stranger in most friendly manner is Hospitality. In most of the countries all over the world a guest is received with a great amount of courtesy and warmth and is provided with entertainment. The basic concept of Hospitality is to make the guest feel that he has come amongst friends and that GUESTS ARE ALWAYS WELCOME. Although the basic concept of hospitality has remained the same, yet with the passage of time and development of technology and science, the needs and wants of travellers have changed greatly thus providing numerous services and facilities in terms of accommodation and other basic needs such as food and beverages. In olden days kings, lords, maharajas, landlords and sometimes the panchayats etc. used to provide food and shelter to travellers and their animals free of charges and it used to be a benevolent activity. But with the passage of time it has not only remained a benevolent activity but has become a flourishing business too.

A part of hospitality activity is being attentive, alert, and cordial with the guest without forcing yourself and your ideas on to him; at the same time being very polite and cooperative. All those working in hospitality industry have one common objective—"Creating an image of friendly reception and treatment" for guests and visitors.

As front office personnel, the hotel staff, in order to provide hospitality should make his guests feel at home and use pleasant tone of voice smilingly, offer his assistance wherever possibly can be provided. Don't ignore the guest, and don't be abrupt no matter how busy you are: anticipate his needs and wants and provide the same without his asking them.

As a hotelier, keep on checking the hospitality attitude of your organization. Make a check list and be sure that you and your staff are fulfilling each and every point of the check list. The check list may include areas such as front desk and lobby, etc. Make sure that the front desk is always kept clean, orderly and well lighted. Even the stationery used is so designed that it does not create confusion and clearly indicates how it is to be filled in, and is inviting. The lobby is kept clean and furniture kept at proper place. Lighting system is soft and appealing.

The welcome spirit that the guest is looking for is there. Floor covering, pictures, furnishing etc. are appealing, attractive and aesthetically designed.

Further, the check list should include the intangibles such as training of the staff and willingness and positive attitude of the staff. The arriving guest is always greeted with a smile and proper salutation to show interest in his trip and his well being.

The hotel industry is, perhaps, one of the oldest commercial endeavours in the world. The first inns go back to the sixth century B.C. and were the products of the urge to travel, spurred by the invention of the 'wheel'. The earliest inns were ventures by husband and wife teams who provided large halls for travellers to make their own beds and sleep on the floor. They also provided modest wholesome food, thirst-quenchers like wine, port, ale, etc. and stabling facilities. Entertainment and recreation were provided by the host's wife or his wench. The entire cooking service, and recreation was provided by the husband and wife team and his family.

These conditions prevailed for several hundred years. The advent of the Industrial Revolution in England brought ideas and progress in the business of innkeeping. The development of railways and steamships made travelling more prominent. The Industrial Revolution also changed travel from social or government travel to business travel. There was a need for quick and clean service.

The lead in hotelkeeping was taken by the emerging nations of Europe, especially Switzerland. It was in Europe that the birth of an organised hotel industry took place in the shape of chalets and small hotels which provided a variety of services and were mainly patronised by the aristocracy of the day.

In early England, public houses were normally called "inns" or "taverns". Normally, the name "inn" was reserved for the finer establishments catering to the nobility and clergy. The houses frequented by the common man were known as "taverns". In France, a similar distinction was made with the finer establishments known as "hotelleries" and the less pretentious houses called "cabarets". The word "hostel" was used after the Norman invasion derived from "host". The "hosteler" was the head of the hostel whereas the same position was called the "innkeeper" in England. The word "hotel" was used in England in about 1760 after a passage of over 80 years. In America lodging houses were called "inn" or "coffee house".

The real growth of the modern hotel industry took place in the USA beginning with the opening of City Hotel in New York in 1794. This was the first building specially erected for hotel purposes. This eventually led to great competition between different cities and resulted in frenzied hotel building activity. Some of the finest hotels of the USA were built in this era, but the real boom in hotel building came in the early twentieth century. This period also saw the beginning of chain operations under the guidance of E.M. Statler. It involved big investments, big profits and trained professionals to manage the business.

GLOBAL CONCEPTS

Pakhtuns

The Pakhtun people of South-Central Asia, pre-dominant in the Khyber Pakhtunkhwa province of Pakistan and Afghanistan have a strong code of hospitality. They are a people characterized by their use of *Pakhtunwali*, an ancient set of ethics, the first principle of which is *Milmastiya* or Hospitality. The general area of Pakhtunistan is also nicknamed *The Land of Hospitality*.

Biblical and Middle Eastern

In Middle Eastern Culture, it was considered a cultural norm to take care of the strangers and foreigners living among you. These norms are reflected in many Biblical commands and examples.

The obligations of both host and guest are stern. The bond is formed by eating salt under the roof, and is so strict that an

Arab story tells of a thief who tasted something to see if it was sugar, and on realizing it was salt, put back all that he had taken and left.

Classical World

To the ancient Greeks and Romans, hospitality was a divine right. The host was expected to make sure the needs of his guests were seen to. The ancient Greek term *xenia,* or *theoxenia* when a god was involved, expressed this ritualized guest-friendship relation.

Celtic Cultures

Celtic societies also valued the concept of hospitality, especially in terms of protection. A host who granted a person's request for refuge was expected not only to provide food and shelter to his/her guest, but to make sure they did not come to harm while under their care.

India

In India, hospitality is based on the principle *Atithi Devo Bhava,* meaning "the guest is God." This principle is shown in a number of stories where a guest is literally a god who rewards the provider of hospitality. From this stems the Indian approach of graciousness towards guests at home, and in all social situations.

CULTURAL VALUE OR NORM

Hospitality as a cultural norm or value is an established sociological phenomenon that people study and write papers about (see references, and Hospitality ethics). Some regions have become stereotyped as exhibiting a particular style of hospitality. Examples include:

- Minnesota nice
- Southern hospitality

Hospitality Service

The concept of **hospitality exchange**, also known as "accommodation sharing", "hospitality services" (short "hospex"), and "home stay networks", refers to centrally organized social networks of individuals, generally travelers, who offer or seek accommodation without monetary exchange. These services generally connect users via the internet.

In 1949, Bob Luitweiler founded the first hospitality service called Servas Open Doors as a cross national, non-profit, volunteer run organization advocating interracial and international peace. In 1965, John Wilcock set up the Traveler's Directory as a listing of his friends willing to host each other when traveling. In 1988, Joy Lily rescued the organization from imminent shutdown, forming Hospitality Exchange. In 1970 Jimmy Carter (then US President) announced the formation of Friendship Force International which has chapters in 57 countries today. In 2000, Veit Kuhne founded Hospitality Club, the first Internet-based service. In 2004, Casey Fenton started CouchSurfing, now the largest hospitality exchange organization.

How they Work

Generally, after registering, members have the option of providing very detailed information and pictures of themselves and of the sleeping accommodation being offered, if any. The more information provided by a member improves the chances that someone will find the member trustworthy enough to be their host or guest. Names and addresses may be verified by volunteers. Members looking for accommodation can search for hosts using several parameters such as age, location, sex, and activity level. Home stays are entirely consensual between the host and guest, and the duration, nature, and terms of the guest's stay are generally worked out in advance to the convenience of both parties. No monetary exchange takes place except under certain circumstances (e.g. the guest may compensate the host for food). After using the service, members can leave a noticeable reference about their host or guest.

Instead of or in addition to accommodation, members also

offer to provide guide services or travel-related advice. The websites of the networks also provide editable travel guides and forums where members may seek travel partners or advice. Many such organizations are also focused on "social networking" and members organize activities such as camping trips, bar crawls, meetings, and sporting events.

Some networks cater to specific niche markets such as students, activists, religious pilgrims, and even occupational groups like police officers.

Benefits

Monetary Savings

As these networks provide accommodation at no charge, monetary savings can be significant.

Local Contact

Hospitality exchange gives travelers the chance to experience what life is like for people living in other places. In addition, making interpersonal connections and fostering understanding of different cultures may in the long run also be important to international relations. During hospitality exchanges, hosts may show off their local knowledge and exciting places "off the tourist map". Not only may travelers get a distinct experience, but they will also get a feel for the everyday lives of local residents.

Reciprocity

The concept behind Hospitality services is based on the pay it forward philosophy, gift economy, and reciprocal altruism.

Drawbacks

Lack of Guarantee

There is no contractual agreement between users in these systems. Reservations are made, but if they are for some reason broken, there is no higher authority to which one could plead for a refund or other compensation. The only repercussion will be the poor rating you give that user and your only consolation will be that your warning will deter others from visiting or hosting them. For those who feel insecure unless their travel arrangements are written in stone before departure, this system will not be comforting.

Potential Interpersonal Conflict or Awkwardness

There is a chance that guest and host will not get along. Perhaps there will be scheduling or ideological conflicts. Maybe you will find that hosts or visitors have misrepresented themselves. Perhaps the experience will not live up to your expectations. Intense interpersonal communications in advance and a flexibility once you have arrived is your best bet. These experiences require additional planning and courtesy towards the demands of your host. Thus, your living conditions, length of stay, and overall experience will be circumscribed by the living conditions you enter into.

Digital Divide and Demographic Segregation

As use of these services generally requires access to the internet and knowledge of the English language, the sample population found in searches of these databases is really much less diverse than a geographical representation of worldwide users might suggest.

Security

Staying in someone's house, or inviting people into your house leaves open the possibility of being taken advantage of.

Example Networks

There are countless websites that serve the idea of hospitality service, with new ones appearing as this phenomenon becomes more popular. While this page is not intended to be a directory listing, here is a small sample of the well-established and long-standing networks:

- CouchSurfing - A very active network with over 2 million members in more than 200 countries
- Friendship Force International A network of chapters worldwide which concentrates on building understanding across cultures.
- Hospitality Club - A very active network with over 550,000 members in more than 200 countries
- Servas International - human rights and global peace oriented since 1949. A relatively small network now with over 15,000 members(?) with a very long history.
- Tripping - A global network of travelers with the motto "For Travelers, Not Tourists"
- BeWelcome

Specialized Networks

Some networks offer specialised hospitality services.

- Lesbian and Gay Hospitality Exchange International
- Warm Showers - Hospitality network for touring cyclists
- Dachgeber - Hospitality network for touring cyclists in Germany with about 3000 members
- Pasporta Servo - for Esperanto speakers.
- WWOOF - "Worldwide Opportunities on Organic Farms", help on the property is exchanged for food, accommodation, education and cultural interaction.
- Freagle - "Free Camping, worldwide!" - Uniting Outdoor Lovers Through Hospitality and Mutual Help.
- HelpX - "Help Exchange", help is exchanged for food, accommodation, experience and cultural interaction.
- Homeshare International - charitable organization providing exchange of housing for help in the home.
- Ridester - ride sharing for travelers in USA.

Southern Hospitality Described

Some characteristics of southern hospitality were described as early as 1835, when Jacob Abbott attributed the poor quality of taverns in the south to the lack of need for them, given the willingness of southerners to provide for strangers.Abbott writes:

" The hospitality of southerners is so profuse, that taverns are but poorly supported. A traveler, with the garb and the manners of a gentleman, finds a welcome at every door. A stranger is riding on horseback through Virginia or Carolina. It is noon. He sees a plantation, surrounded with trees, a little distance from the road. Without hesitation he rides to the door. The gentleman of the house sees his approach and is ready upon the steps."

Abbot further describes how the best stores of the house are at the disposal of visitors.Furthermore, says Abbott:

"Conversation flows cheeringly, for the southern gentleman has a particular tact in making a guest happy. After dinner you are urged to pass the afternoon and night, and if you are a gentleman in manners and information, your host will be in reality highly gratified by your so doing.Such is the character of southern hospitality."

Food figures highly in Southern hospitality, a large component of the idea being the provision of Southern cuisine to visitors. A cake or other delicacy is often brought to the door of a new neighbor as a mechanism of introduction. Many club and church functions include a meal or at least a dessert and beverage. Churches in the South frequently have large commercial style kitchens to accommodate this tradition, but many "fellowship suppers" are "covered dish": everyone attending brings a dish. However, if a newcomer arrives without a dish, he or she will be made to feel welcome and served generously. When a death or serious illness occurs, neighbors, friends, and church members generally bring food to the bereaved family for a period of time. A number of cookbooks promise recipes advancing this concept.

Other features of Southern Hospitality include proper local etiquette (i.e., calling one "Sir" or "Ma'am," opening doors for women (as well as men removing their hats when in the presence of a woman or inside her house), cooking enough for everyone who might be around at mealtime, inviting one to church functions, etc.) While persons from outside the region often mistake many of the southern hospitality customs as being disingenuous or fake in some way, in actuality the customs are often a way to make the visitor feel as comfortable as possible in an unfamiliar setting. Additionally, although some customs may be seen as odd or even offensive by people not from the South, they are considered polite in local culture and usually meant as an expression of traditional warm greeting.

Critical Examination

Southern hospitality has been examined by sociologists and other social scientists, one of whom has characterized the practices as a masquerade designed to cover deficiencies in southern culture, such as slavery, discrimination, and widespread poverty. Southern hospitality has also been examined, however, as a reflection of the deeply-held religious beliefs of the region; the idea that one should be good to strangers is an outgrowth of such Biblical parables as the Good Samaritan. Indeed Ernest Hamlin Abbott wrote in 1902, "as religious observances are in the South as naturally included in the hospitality of the home as anything else, so, conversely, hospitality in the South is an integral part of the church services".

Tourism and Hospitality

As per the Travel and Tourism Competitiveness Report 2009 by the World Economic Forum, India is ranked 11th in the Asia Pacific region and 62nd overall, moving up three places on the list of the world's attractive destinations. It is ranked the 14th best tourist destination for its natural resources and 24th for its cultural resources, with many World Heritage sites, both natural and cultural, rich fauna, and strong creative industries in the country. India also bagged 37th rank for its air transport network. The India travel and tourism industry ranked 5th in the long-term (10-year) growth and is expected to be the second largest employer in the world by 2019.

Contribution to the Economy

Combining unparalleled growth prospects and unlimited business potential, the industry is certainly on the foyer towards being a key player in the nation's changing face. Furthermore, banking on the government's initiative of upgrading and expanding the country's infrastructure like airports, national highways etc, the tourism and hospitality industry is bound to get a bounce in its growth.

The hotel and tourism industry's contribution to the Indian economy by way of foreign direct investments (FDI) inflows were pegged at US$ 2.24 billion from April 2000 to November 2010, according to the Department of Industrial Policy and Promotion (DIPP).

India's hotel pipeline is the second largest in the Asia-Pacific region according to Jan Smits, Regional Managing Director, Inter Continental Hotels Group (IHG) Asia Australasia. He added that the Indian hospitality industry is projected to grow at a rate of 8.8 per cent during 2007-16, placing India as the second-fastest growing tourism market in the world. Initiatives like massive investment in hotel infrastructure and open-sky policies made by the government are all aimed at propelling growth in the hospitality sector.

Foreign Tourist Arrivals

Ministry of Tourism compiles monthly estimates of Foreign Tourist Arrivals (FTAs) in India and Foreign Exchange Earnings (FEE) from tourism on the basis of data received from major airports. Following are the important highlights, as regards these two important indicators of tourism sector for 2010 and December 2010.

- FTAs in India during 2010 were 5.58 million with a

growth rate of 9.3 per cent as compared to the FTAs of 5.11 million during 2009.

- FTAs during the December 2010 was 6,55,000 as compared to FTAs of 6,46,000 in December 2009 and 5,34,000 in December 2008.
- FEE from tourism during 2010 were US$ 14,193 million as compared to US$ 11.39 billion during 2009 and US$ 11.74 billion during 2008. The growth rate in FEE in US$ terms during 2010 was 24.6 per cent.
- FEE from tourism during the month of December during 2010 were US$ 1.55 billion.

HOSPITALITY INDUSTRY

The **hospitality industry** consists of broad category of fields within the service industry that includes lodging, restaurants, event planning, theme parks, transportation, cruise line, and additional fields within the tourism industry. The hospitality industry is a several billion dollar industry that mostly depends on the availability of leisure time and disposable income. A hospitality unit such as a restaurant, hotel, or even an amusement park consists of multiple groups such as facility maintenance, direct operations (servers, housekeepers, porters, kitchen workers, bartenders, etc.), management, marketing, and human resources. The hospitality industry covers a wide range of organizations offering food service and accommodation. The hospitality industry is divided into sectors according to the skill-sets required for the work involved. Sectors include accommodation, food and beverage, meeting and events, gaming, entertainment and recreation, tourism services, and visitor information.

Usage rate is an important variable for the hospitality industry. Just as a factory owner would wish to have his or her productive asset in use as much as possible (as opposed to having to pay fixed costs while the factory isn't producing), so do restaurants, hotels, and theme parks seek to maximize the number of customers they "process" in all sectors. This led to formation of services with the aim to increase usage rate provided by hotel consolidators. Information about required or offered products are brokered on business networks used by vendors as well as purchasers.

In viewing various industries, "barriers to entry" by newcomers and competitive advantages between current players are very important. Among other things, hospitality industry players find advantage in old classics (location), initial and ongoing investment support (reflected in the material upkeep of facilities and the luxuries located therein), and particular themes adopted by the marketing arm of the organization in question (such as a restaurant called the 51st fighter group that has a WW2 theme in music and other environmental aspects). Very important is also the characteristics of the personnel working in direct contact with the customers. The authenticity, professionalism, and actual concern for the happiness and well-being of the customers that is communicated by successful organizations is a clear competitive advantage.

EVENT MANAGEMENT

Event management is the application of project management to the creation and development of festivals, events and conferences.

Event management involves studying the intricacies of the brand, identifying the target audience, devising the event concept, planning the logistics and coordinating the technical aspects before actually executing the modalities of the proposed event. Post-event analysis and ensuring a return on investment have become significant drivers for the event industry.

The recent growth of festivals and events as an industry around the world means that the management can no longer be *ad hoc*. Events and festivals, such as the Asian Games, have a large impact on their communities and, in some cases, the whole country.

The industry now includes events of all sizes from the Olympics down to a breakfast meeting for ten business people. Many industries, charitable organizations, and interest groups will hold events of some size in order to market themselves, build business relationships, raise money or celebrate.

Services

Event management companies and organizations service a variety of areas including corporate events (product launches, press conferences, corporate meetings and conferences), marketing programs (road shows, grand opening events), and special corporate hospitality events like concerts, award ceremonies, film premieres, launch/release parties, fashion shows, commercial events, private (personal) events such as weddings and bar mitzvahs.

Clients hire event management companies to handle a specific scope of services for the given event, which at its maximum may include all creative, technical and logistical elements of the event. (Or just a subset of these, depending on the client's needs, expertise and budget).

Event manager

The event manager is the person who plans and executes the event. Event managers and their teams are often behind-the-scenes running the event. Event managers may also be involved in more than just the planning and execution of the event, but also brand building, marketing and communication strategy. The event manager is an expert at the creative, technical and logistical elements that help an event succeed. This includes event design, audio-visual production, scriptwriting, logistics, budgeting, negotiation and, of course, client service. It is a multi-dimensional profession.

The event manager may become involved at the early initiation stages of the event. If the event manager has budget responsibilities at this early stage they may be termed an event or production executive. The early stages include:

- Site surveying

- Client Service
- Brief clarification
- Budget drafting
- Cash flow management
- Supply chain identification
- Procurement
- Scheduling
- Site design
- Technical design
- Health & Safety

An event manager who becomes involved closer to the event will often have a more limited brief. The key disciplines closer to the event are:

- Health & Safety including crowd management,
- Logistics
- Rigging
- Sound
- Light
- Video
- Detailed scheduling
- Security

As an Industry

Event Management is a multi-million dollar industry, growing rapidly, with mega shows and events hosted regularly. Surprisingly, there is no formalized research conducted to assess the growth of this industry. The industry includes fields such as the MICE (Meetings, Incentives, Conventions and Exhibitions), conferences and seminars as well as live music and sporting events.

The logistics side of the industry is paid less than the sales/ sponsorship side, though some may say that these are two different industries.

Technology

Event management software companies provide event planners with software tools to handle many common activities such as delegate registration, hotel booking, travel booking or allocation of exhibition floorspace.

Education

There are an increasing number of universities which offer courses in event management, including diplomas and graduate degrees. In addition to these academic courses, there are many associations and societies that provide courses on the various aspects of the industry. Study includes organizational skills, technical knowledge, P.R., marketing, advertising, catering, logistics, decor, glamor identity, human relations, study of law and licenses, risk management, budgeting, study of allied industries like television, other media and several other areas. Certification can be acquired from various sources to obtain designations such as Certified Trade Show Marketer (CTSM), Certified Manager of Exhibits (CME), Certified in Exhibition Management (CEM), Global Certification in Meeting Management (CMM), Certified Meeting Professional (CMP) and the Certified Special Event Professional (CSEP).

Career opportunities are in the following Industries :

1. Event Management
2. Event Management Consultancy
3. Hotel, travel and hospitality Industries
4. Advertising Agencies
5. Public Relations Firms
6. Corporations
7. News Media
8. Non-profit organization
9. Integrated Marketing & Communications

10. Event Budgeting and Accounting

Categories of Events

Events can be classified into four broad categories based on their purpose and objective:

1. Leisure events e.g. leisure sport, music, recreation.
2. Cultural events e.g. ceremonial, religious, art, heritage, and folklore.
3. Personal events e.g. weddings, birthdays, anniversaries.
4. Organizational events e.g. commercial, political, charitable, sales, product launch,expo.

CORPORATE ENTERTAINMENT

Corporate entertainment relates to private events held by corporations or businesses for their staff, clients or stakeholders. These events can be for large audiences such as conventions and conferences, or smaller events such as retreats, Christmas parties or even private concerts. It is also commonly used to mean corporate hospitality, the process of entertaining guests at corporate events. The companies that provides corporate entertainment are called Corporate Event Planners or Corporate Booking Agencies.

CORPORATE ENTERTAINMENT, HOSPITALITY & CORPORATE EVENT MANAGEMENT

We specialise in corporate entertainment and corporate event management. We have organised more than 5,000 professional Corporate Events since 1989. Team building events are always popular and we have many satisfied clients who have taken part in both outdoor and indoor team building events. We offer a range of activites such as Crystal Maze themed days, Team Drumming, It's A Knockout and Family Fun Days. Treasure Hunts are versatile events and we often combine these with corporate entertainment in London, which is an excellent location and convenient for many. One way that we do this is to combine the Treasure Hunt with a Thames rib power boat chase. We offer a whole host of themes, including 007 themed parties and Fun Casino evenings. These types of activities are very popular in the corporate entertainment industry.

The Corporate Entertainment Company Ltd

The Corporate Entertainment Company has been the UK's leading supplier of official corporate hospitality at major sporting events for over 10 years.

Whether you plan to entertain clients or reward your staff, The Corporate Entertainment Company will provide you with a service that sets us apart from our competitors. We pride ourselves on offering an honest and 'real' appraisal of events and a level of attention to detail that ensures you meet all of your expectations AND your commercial objectives.

By adhering to the strictest codes of practice within the industry and offering only the very best in official hospitality, we have developed an extensive list of clients who return to us on a regular basis in the knowledge that we are part of their team.

Please navigate to a preferred sport or participation event using the menu to your left. Alternatively, please contact us directly on 01825 760065 and speak to one of our advisers.

Rendezvous at the luxurious Oakley Court Hotel and enjoy a relaxing stroll through the beautiful hotel grounds to the jetty. Climb aboard your private river cruiser and relish an hour long journey to Windsor Racecourse, taking in the amazing sights including Windsor Castle from the river. Experience the finest hospitality and the unique atmosphere of Windsor Racecourse prior to your return river cruise to the Oakley Court Hotel. There you can relax and enjoy the extensive facilities the hotel has to offer, including a luxurious overnight stay with breakfast.

Three unique experiences all rolled into one – and all with an eye on the budget!

For a truly classic occasion, entertain your guests in the luxury of our Private Box at Ascot. Now available for a selection of the remaining 2010 fixtures, our box is located centrally within the new Grandstand and accommodates 8 for a sit down and 18 for a buffet. With views over the final furlong, your guests will receive hospitality of the highest quality whilst enjoying the exciting closing moments of each race. From as little as £165.00 + VAT per person for a two-course meal including unlimited beers, wines and soft drinks, this represents excellent value for money.

Celebrate Christmas in style as three of London's most famous attractions transform into London's top Xmas Party venues. Madame Tussauds, the Sealife London Aquarium and the London Dungeons offer the perfect solutions to your Xmas Party requirements - great entertainment, good food, spectacular surroundings and a truly unique atmosphere!

For all racing enthusiasts, the final English Classic of the year, the St Leger, is run at Doncaster in September. At a time when the sporting calendar is relatively light on attractions, we can offer amazing hospitality in either marquees or private executive boxes at one of the most prestigious race meetings of the year.

Sample some of the finest football hospitality at Chelsea, Manchester United, Liverpool and Spurs for the 2010 / 2011 season. With luxurious facilities and first class seating, you and your guests are certain to enjoy the experience.

England's rugby team take on their southern hemisphere rivals in a series of Autumn Internationals in November. New Zealand, Australia, Samoa and South Africa face an England side in transition following mixed fortunes in the 2010 RBS Six Nations Championship. Experience the excitement of these fixtures from top quality seating with luxurious hospitality within the Orchard Enclosure.

Package Holiday

A **package holiday** or **package tour** consists of transport and accommodation advertised and sold together by a vendor known as a tour operator. Other services may be provided like a rental car, activities or outings during the holiday. Transport can be via charter airline to a foreign country. Package holidays are a form of product bundling.

Package holidays are organised by a tour operator and sold to a consumer by a travel agent. Some travel agents are employees of tour operators, others are independent.

Package Tours

An early form of package holiday was organised by Thomas Cook in 1841, offering customers a return trip between Leicester and Loughborough. The first package tour of Europe was organised by Cook in 1855, and by 1872 he was undertaking world-wide tours, albeit with small groups.

Vladimir Raitz, the co-founder of the Horizon Holiday Group, pioneered the first mass package holidays abroad with charter flights between Gatwick airport and Corsica in 1950, and organised the first package holiday to Palma in 1952, Lourdes in 1953, and the Costa Brava and Sardinia in 1954. In addition, the amendments made in Montreal to the Convention on International Civil Aviation on June 14, 1954 was very liberal to Spain, allowing impetus for mass tourism using charter planes.

By the late 1950s and 1960s, these cheap package holidays — which combined flight, transfers and accommodation — provided the first chance for most people in the United Kingdom to have affordable travel abroad. One of the first charter airlines was Euravia, which commenced flights from Manchester Airport in 1961 and Luton Airport in 1962. Despite opening up mass tourism to Crete and the Algarve in 1970, the package tour industry declined during the 1970s. On 15 August 1974, the industry was shaken when the second-largest tour operator, Court Line which operated under the brand names of Horizon and Clarksons, collapsed. Nearly 50,000 tourists were stranded overseas and a further 100,000 faced the loss of booking deposits.

In 2005 a growing number of consumers were avoiding package holidays and were instead travelling with budget airlines and booking their own accommodation. In the UK, the downturn in the package holiday market led to the consolidation of the tour operator market, which is now dominated by a few large tour operators. The major operators are Thomson Holidays and First Choice part of TUI AG and Thomas Cook AG. Under these umbrella brands there exists a whole range of different holiday operators catering to different markets, such as Club 18-30 or Simply Travel. Budget airlines have also created their own package holiday divisions such as Jet2 Holidays.

The trend for package holiday bookings saw a comeback in 2009, as customers sought greater financial security in the wake of a number of holiday and flight companies going bust, and as the hidden costs of 'no-frills' flights increased. Coupled with the search for late holidays as holidaymakers left booking to the last moment, this led to a rise in consumers booking package holidays.

Dynamic Packaging

Dynamic packaging is a method that is becoming increasingly used in package holiday booking procedures that enables consumers to build their own package of flights, accommodation and hire car instead of a pre-defined package.

Free Independent Traveler

Free Independent Traveler (or Tourist) refers to both a way of traveling and, from an industry viewpoint, a sector within the tourism market. FITs practise a form of dynamic packaging but the emphasis is from the end-user point of view and includes the wider economic effects that FITs "spread" in their destination country as opposed to more traditional, consolidated forms of travel.

Corporate Hospitality

The companies listed in the 'Corporate Hospitality' section

of Partyoffers are there to assist and advise in choosing the solution to match the client's needs in this important corporate sector. Corporate hospitality events are held at a huge range of venues with different packages available depending on the client's budget and the type of hospitality and entertainment required.

Popular choices of venue include sporting events, theatre and opera. Tickets for these events are often hard to obtain, this is where the specialists are able to help. The choice of events providing sports hospitality packages is extremely varied with such entertainment available at Premier and Champions League football matches, horse racecourses including Royal Ascot and The Cheltenham Gold Cup, Test and county cricket matches, Grand Prix circuits and tennis tournaments including Wimbledon. You can also make use of a venue finding service to advise you on the suitability and availability of venues for corporate hospitaility.

Event Services

The 'Event Services' category pages of the Partyoffers directory cover the broad range of services that are necessary to put on an event. These services are the bricks and mortar that make the whole occasion possible and are an essential sector of the UK events industry. Companies and individuals wishing to hold a corporate event or private party need look no further than this section of our directory which serves as a one-stop shop providing details of every type of service provider that you might possibly need to enable the event to take place. For those who are looking to organize the event themselves, we list suppliers of a diverse selection of services including portable toilet, marquee and catering equipment hire companies to help keep your guests comfortable, portable dancefloor hire companies to keep them dancing and laser, lightshow and firework display organisers to keep them entertained. We also list event management companies and party organisers throughout the United Kingdom who excel at coordinating the entire event, taking control of all the hassle and logistics of putting the show on the road.

Clicking on your required choice of event service will take you to a specific page listing the individual service providers and event management companies providing the service you require. The category pages within this section of Partyoffers also advise you of similar categories which may be relevant to your search.

The 'Event Services' category pages often contain links to articles that we publish. These articles, written by companies that we list and ourselves, are there to provide information and assist in enabling you to choose the most ideally suited form of service for your event. Whether you are looking to book promotional staff for a corporate event or an ice sculpture for a wedding, you can be sure to find the event service provider suited to your event in the 'Event Services' pages of the Partyoffers nationwide online events directory.

Corporate Events

Corporate Events involve many aspects including corporate event management, corporate event entertainment, event venue finding services, team building and corporate hospitality - to name just a few. In these pages of Partyoffers you will find the cream of corporate events management companies specialising in organising London corporate events as well as corporate events throughout the UK.

INTERNATIONAL HOSPITALITY FAIR IN UK

London is a city that has always embraced different cultures and traditions keeping its individuality intact. Whatever time of the year, there are always festival events in London. The high spirits, celebrations and the excitement amongst the people of the city make the London festivals an unforgettable experience.

The music and dance shows, the food festivals in London, innumerable parties and the fireworks happening in the most renowned venues of the city terms London as a festival city.

Taste of London—Hotly anticipated London restaurant event Taste of London 2010 brings together a selection of world famous London restaurants in an unique outdoors food and drink festival, showcasing cuisine from some of the country's best chefs. In conjunction with Channel 4 and in partnership with British Airways, the Taste of London festival will enable visitors to sample gourmet cooking in Regents Park over four mouthwatering days in June. Tasty stuff.

World class cuisine—Plenty of famous London restaurants will be participating in the food festival at Regents Park this year, serving up a selection of dishes for visitors to sample and enjoy, making Taste of London 2010 a food event that no self respecting London foodie would dream of missing. When it comes to London restaurant events, Taste of London certainly wins hands down. Cooking from across the globe will feature at the food festival in Regents Park as the flagship event of the national Taste Festivals returns to London in 2010.

Celebrity chefs from London restaurants:A line up of renowned chefs are represented at the 2010 festival. Chefs from well known restaurants and TV shows that are gracing Regents Park include Michel Roux Jr, Vivek Singh, Gary Rhodes, Tristan Welch, Richard Corrigan, Anna Hansen and Theo Randall. The 2010 London restaurants set to make your mouth water include Asia de Cuba, Tamarind, The Cinnamon Club, Fino, Club Gascon, Gaucho, Maze, Odette's, Tom's Kitchen, Satay House, Bentleys Oyster bar and Grill, Min Jiang and The Modern Pantry, perfect for hungry restaurant hunters out for lunch.

Sample some of the best—With a whole host of restaurants here in miniature, visitors to this fantastic London restaurant event can sample signature dishes from some of the most exclusive London restaurants, freshly cooked at mini kitchens on site and served up at a fraction of the price you would pay for the full sized dish at their restaurants.

Try something new—In addition to world class London restaurants and gourmet cooking, a range of speciality foods and ingredients will be available to buy at the food festival. Expert chefs will be on hand to explain their creations and answer any questions, whilst workshops and interactive demonstrations give you the chance to have a go on the day and make it a London restaurant event with an added interactive element.

Have a drink—If you work up a thirst sampling all that food and roaming Regents Park, special drink academies will also be open throughout the festival. Visit the Taste Wine experience or a Champagne masterclass for a refreshing sip before heading back to the kitchens for more food.

Spend a Crown or two—The official currency of the festival is the Crown, each of which is worth 50p. Crowns can be bought in advance with your ticket or obtained at the food festival and signature dish prices average around nine Crowns. So pack your appetite and get spending!

Taste of Malaysia—Fans of Malaysian cuisine will be in seventh heaven as Taste of Malaysia comes to the 2010 festival. You'll be able to indulge in a culinary journey through the different foods of Malaysia with demonstrations, performances and highlight dishes from top Malaysian restaurants. And just to really make the Taste of Malaysia arena appealing, Rick Stein will be the official ambassador, on hand to show his expert knowledge of Asian cuisine with demonstrations, advice and more.

The 2010 festival took place at Regents Park from Thursday 17th June - Sunday 20th June 2010. Times run from 12pm - 4pm and 5.30pm - 9.30pm Thursday - Saturday, and 12pm - 5pm Sunday.Tickets for the London restaurant event cost £22.00 - £75.00.

ST PATRICK'S DAY 2011 IN LONDON

Celebrate St Patrick's Day 2011 in London by joining in the St Patrick's Day parade, the largest London festival event in Britain! The 'Paddys' day parade begins at 12 noon and will follow the route from Park Lane to Hyde Park Corner, down Piccadilly onto Regent Street by Trafalgar Square and dispersing into Whitehall Place.

The streets of London on St Patricks Day '11 will be transformed into a merry crowd including a full parade of floats, marching bands, stilt walkers, costume characters, street theatre and dancers. As the St Patrick's Day Parade makes its way through central London, people can enjoy superb performances and live music along the route.

Finally, the London parade will join the St Patrick's Day festival, which will be celebrated in Leicester Square, Covent Garden and Trafalgar Square from 12 noon to 6 pm. Trafalgar Square will be a base for both time-honoured and contemporary Irish entertainment; with crafts, dance and music creating a vibrant atmosphere. The greatest Irish travel exhibition in Britain will be on show, tempting you to travel to the Emerald Isle.

In Covent Garden, be sure to indulge on Irish treats at the Irish specialty food market, open over St Patricks Day weekend. Plenty of delicious food and drink will be on sale, giving Londoners a taste of Irish traditions and reminding expats what they're missing in Ireland. In Leicester Square, this will be your chance to learn the Irish dance Ceili. The St Patrick's Day parade and festival in London make an excellent day out for families and are a great chance for all Londoners, Irish and non-Irish alike, to celebrate. It assures to be a fun filled day with various activities from parade, food market, music and dance for the whole family and all types of friend.

SCI FI FILM FESTIVAL IN LONDON

Sci Fi London is an international science fiction and fantasy film festival in London. Focusing on the creative genre, Sci Fi London Film Festival celebrates films and books with leading reviews, forums and news. Sci Fi Film Festival '11 in London covers every aspect of the Sci Fi world. This Sci Fi event in London, started by its director Louis Savy, has become a highly anticipated and prominent event in the film calendar.

Described as a "festival for people who don't like Sci Fi", this particular event promises to attract a wide number of people with different interests and tastes, not just the strange Star Trek addicts. Targeted but open to everyone, The Sci Fi London Film Festival is a chance for some to discover the great things about science fiction! With Harry Potter's fantastic success, as well as the recent boom in Comic book films over the last decade, not to mention Lord of the Rings; fantasy films and science fiction have never been more popular.

Each Sci Fi Film Festival in London offers several UK primary concerts. This Sci Fi London Film Festival will acquire position on 14th - 16th October '11 by numerous London locations counting The Apollo West End Cinema. Alongside the standard pictures encoding (which contain shorts, character, documentaries & globe primary concert) the London film festival will feature a sequence of conference and question listed sort narrative, pictures & television.

The Sci Fi Film Festival '11 in London will display pictures for more than three days and thousands of visitors will attend. Escape the real world by heading to Sci Fi London!

CITY OF LONDON FESTIVAL 2011

The City of London Festival 2011 is a major highlight of London's cultural calendar. Held every summer, this London festival animates the special structures and unique spaces of the City. St Paul's Cathedral, churches, squares and other areas are decorated with diverse, creative and inventive schemes ranging across film, music, visual arts and other media.

The City of London Festival '11 is a fantastic offering of free cultural events. You can listen to live jazz, see an exclusive exhibition or watch a street-theatre surrounding by iconic landmarks. There are more than 100 free outdoor events every year and about 50 ticketed concerts.

The City of London Festival was founded in 1962 to revitalize the cultural life in the city. Today, the London festival is booming, popular with Londoners and foreign visitors alike. Widely broadcast by the BBC and publicised in the press, the City of London Festival '11 promises a great time for every kind of art-lover.

London Festival entertains and refreshes the City's workers, residents and visitors with special events and world-class artists in beautiful surroundings. There is no better chance to get to know London. Don't miss the City of London Festival '11 this summer!

NOTTING HILL CARNIVAL 2011 LONDON

Ever since from 1964, the Notting Hill Carnival in London, Notting Hill is amazingly developing into the Europe's leading festival of its own type, offering two full days of fun, music and dance. Held annually in August, the Notting Hill Carnival makes the West London's streets alive with the vibrations of Europe's largest street festival.

Bright and attractive costumes colour the exciting Carnival parade, which spans over three miles of Notting Hill London's main street, and fascinates a number of visitors to join this yearly street party in London's most eventful place and also attracts hundreds of full-blooded groups from South America, Africa and Caribbean region to join in the Notting Hill Carnival 2011 in London.

Exciting with quite a few Caribbean food stands, a range of dynamic sound systems, millions of carnival lovers and thousands of volunteers, the Notting Hill Carnival '11 in London is now become a vigorous carnival that continues to draw attention of millions of tourists from all corners of the world. For food-lovers, this splendid carnival in London's Notting Hill offers an exciting choice with jerk chicken, rice and peas, and rum punch as well as the unusual flavour of many other mouth-watering cuisines.

Enjoy the sight of fantastically dressed dancers, steelbands, calypso and soca musicians, and large sound systems are joined by more than a million party goers from the whole world and of all ages at the Notting Hill Carnival '11 in London.

Decide your favourite spot early ahead of visiting this jam-packed and fun-filled street festival - the Notting Hill Carnival in London.

LONDON MELA 2011

London Mela 2011 will be held at Gunnersbury Park in Ealing London this August, and is all set to explore diverse colours of the flourishing South Asian culture with nine exciting zones. This year's mela holds an impressive line-up of international stars and vibrant performers, coming together from every corner of the world and making a whole park alive with the dances, theatre and traditional performances.

London Mela '11 in Gunnersbury Park fascinates music savvy people with a huge variety of music, ranging from the time-honoured classical music to the trendy modern music. Various devoted zones for DJs, dance, street arts, comedy, and visual arts are also on hand at this multi-coloured mela. Other highlights of London Mela include the amazing diversity of food, carefully selected from South Asia as well as the whole world and most of all, an interesting fairground area with rides and thrills, perfect for all the ages.

A Multicultural London Mela celebrates Asian culture and music and receives over 50,000 visits per year. London Mela '11 will offer numerous stages for all types of amusement - from conventional pop to long-standing classical music, sophisticated urban grooves and interesting East/West fusion, there will be certainly something for everyone! London Mela will feature heritage attractions, exciting dance performances, kids' and sports activities, long-established craft stalls and a massive funfair and an astonishing carnival-style finale in Gunnersbury Park, Ealing London!

New Challenges for Britain

Life's winners and losers were laid bare today in an official report by the Equality and Human Rights Commission into how fair Britain has become.

The commission's first three-year review, How Fair is Britain, shows that while some inequalities remain entrenched, new challenges are emerging as the country's population becomes older and more ethnically and religiously diverse.

The study identifies "five great gateways" to opportunity – revolving around well-being, education, work, security and voice in society – where millions could benefit if barriers are lifted. These should become the basis to assess "fairness" in public policy, the commission says.

In health, the report says, the poorest can expect to live seven years less than the richest. In education, boys are falling far behind with girls outperforming them at ages 5, 16 and degree level. Students of Indian and Chinese origin are streaking ahead at school.

In criminal justice, Gypsy and traveller communities appear to be targeted – and women prisoners have become a prominent feature of Britain's jails. The ageing society means that women have a 50% chance of becoming a carer before they reach 59.

Trevor Phillips, chair of the commission, says in the 21st century there are still "gateways to opportunity that appear permanently closed, no matter how hard they try; while others seem to have been issued with an 'access all areas' pass at birth".

These distinctions are more nuanced than in the past. Race matters, but so does heritage. Ethnic differences at GCSE are narrowing, except for the top end where the two highest performing groups are students of Chinese and Indian origin.

Free school meals, given only to those on low incomes in Britain, are a strong indicator of class distinctions even at the upper levels of performance. The highest performing group in England are Chinese girls, with even those on free school meals outranking every other group's "educational development" – except better-off Chinese girls.

In employment, a quarter of men of Pakistani descent drive for a living – mostly in a taxi cab.

"There's good news for some ethnic minorities who perhaps prioritise education," said John Hills, professor of social policy at the London School of Economics, who chaired the last government's National Equality Panel report. "At the same time we are seeing a huge amount of self-employment in other groups, such as Pakistani men. There's evidence to suggest that discrimination in the recruitment process keeps them out of jobs."

Prof Hills said that the report showed "we can both be upbeat and also know how far we have to go ... which is hugely important given that the equal opportunity society has been put at the heart of the [coalition] government."

The commission does say that Britain is a largely "tolerant and open-minded society", which has become more socially liberal in recent decades. Opposition to working for an ethnic minority boss and aversion to mixed-race marriages has dropped. Gone too are the stereotypical views about the roles that men and women should play in family.

The study says the biggest change has been the dramatic shift in attitudes to homosexuality. "A gap of less than 20 years separated the parliamentary debates about Section 28 [which banned councils from 'promoting' homosexuality] and civil partnership."

This is not to say that Britons are not worried by the speed and direction of change in the country. The commission says this is best exemplified by the "immigration paradox": three-quarters of Britons say that they are concerned about the scale of immigration at a national level – about the same proportion feels that immigration is not a problem for their own communities.

There is also an acceptance that however far we have travelled towards being a fairer society at ease with itself, substantial evidence shows Britons get neither equal outcomes nor equal chances.

From the cradle to the grave, race, religion, class, disability and gender can all have a bearing on a person's prospects. But explanations are never simple: the report shows that black Caribbean and Pakistani babies are twice as likely to die in their first year than white British babies – yet Bangladeshi babies survive as long as their white peers.

While disabilities often mean lower income levels and life expectancy, the commission finds that "being black and male appears to have a greater impact on levels of numeracy than being learning disabled". In terms of geography, the commission says that "one in four Welsh adults lack basic literacy skills, more than in any English region and in contrast to one in six in England overall".

The gender pay gap remains – men earn 16% more than women on average and "progress appears to be grinding to a halt". But there are significant differences among women. Those with degrees are estimated to face only a 4% loss in lifetime earnings as a result of motherhood, while mothers with no qualifications suffer a 58% loss.

Disabled groups said they were concerned how, given such degrees of disadvantage, the government could target vulnerable people with spending cuts. Richard Hawkes, chief executive of disability charity Scope, said: "If disabled people in their early 20s are twice as likely not to be in employment, education or training, then we question the wisdom of the government's plans to strip away employment support services to the tune of £4.87bn over the next five years."

One of the most shocking revelations, given the acceptance of homosexuality in adult life, was the level of homophobic bullying found in schools. The commission found that two-thirds of "lesbian, gay and transgender" secondary students report that they have been victims of often severe bullying – 17% of those bullied reported having received death threats.

"It is a very worrying statistic," said a spokesman for Stonewall, the gay and lesbian rights group. "We have seen a number of recent high-profile homophobic hate crimes, including assault, where the attackers have been schoolchildren or school leavers."

Another worrying feature of crime in Britain is the prevalence of rape – and the low rate of conviction. There has been no significant fall in the level of rape or serious sexual assault recorded in the British crime survey over the last five years. Over a quarter of all rapes reported to the police in England and Wales last year were committed against children aged under 16, while that figure rose to over half for male rapes.

The review acknowledges it is not definitive. It admits to "significant gaps in knowledge and data" about particular groups, such as transgender people.

A spokesman for the Government Equalities Office said: "When people are treated fairly, everyone in society benefits. That's why this government is committed to tackling all forms of inequality and discrimination, and we welcome the EHRC's contribution to the debate. We will be studying the review's conclusions carefully."

Restaurant Show London 2010

The Restaurant Show London 2010 took place at Earls Court 2 from 11th to 13th October.

Visitors to this year's restaurant show feasted their eyes, ears, and taste buds on the new and exciting products available to shake up their offering.

By visiting the Show, you came away with the one product or idea that can make the biggest difference to your business. If you work for, with or in an independent restaurant, a restaurant chain, a gastro pub, a contract caterer, a bar or a hotel group, then you cannot afford to miss The Restaurant Show 2010.

The Restaurant Show was more than an exhibition - it's a day out. The visitors saw over 350 major suppliers, source new products, visit our inspirational features and see talks and demonstrations. Next time, don't waste your valuable time anywhere else!

Destinations: The Holiday & Travel Show

Venue: Earls Court One **Event type:** Consumer

Web: www.destinationsshow.com **Dates:** 02-05 February 2012

Times:

Thursday: 10am-8.30pm

Friday: 10am-5.30pm

Saturday: 10am-5.30pm

Sunday: 10am-5.30pm

The Times presents Destinations: The Holiday & Travel Show which will be returning to NEC, Birmingham once again in 2011. Guest speakers at the Show in the Meet the Experts Theatre will include Simon Reeve, Ben Anderson and Mark Carwardine. Here, we will give brief biographies of all these personalities, so that readers of all over the world can get some idea of their lifestyle and achievements.

SIMON REEVE (UK TELEVISION PRESENTER)

Reeve was born on 1972 and brought up in west London, and attended a local comprehensive school. He has said his childhood holidays were usually in Dorset, England, and that he rarely went abroad until he started work.

He is a British author, adventurer and TV presenter. Based in London, he makes travel documentaries in little-known areas of the world and has written books on international terrorism, modern history and about his adventures. Reeve has been around the world three times for the BBC television series Tropic of Cancer, Equator, and Tropic of Capricorn, and has travelled extensively in more than 90 countries, including troubled states in Africa, the Caucasus, Latin America, Eastern Europe, the Middle East, Far East and Central Asia.Reeve is the *New York Times* bestselling author of *The New Jackals* (1998), *One Day in September* (2000) and *Tropic of Capricorn* (2007). He has received a One World Broadcasting Trust Award for an "outstanding contribution to greater world understanding."

After leaving school Reeve took a series of jobs, including working in a supermarket, a jewellery shop, and a charity shop, before he started researching and writing in his spare time while working as a postboy at a British newspaper. Reeve then conducted investigations into subjects such as arms-dealing, nuclear smuggling, terrorism and organized crime before he began studying the 1993 World Trade Center bombing just days after the attack. Reeve's research formed the basis for his book *The New Jackals: Ramzi Yousef, Osama bin Laden and the future of terrorism*. Published in the UK and USA in the late 1990s, *The New Jackals* was the first book on bin Laden. Classified information cited by Reeve detailed the existence, development, and aims of the terrorist group al-Qaeda.

The book warned that al-Qaeda was planning huge attacks on the West, and concluded that an apocalyptic terrorist strike by the group was almost inevitable. It has been a *New York Times* bestseller , and in the three months after the 9/11 attacks it was one of the top three bestselling books in the United States. After the 9/11 attacks Reeve became a regular commentator and reference source on the emerging terror threat. He has been quoted in *The New York Times* warning that al-Qaeda was moving "far beyond being a terrorist organization to being almost a state of mind. That's terribly significant because it gives the movement a scope and longevity it didn't have before 9/11."

Reeve followed *The New Jackals* with a study of the 1972 Munich massacre called *One Day in September: the full story of the 1972 Munich Olympics massacre and the Israeli revenge operation 'Wrath of God'*, published in 2000 by Faber & Faber. The book detailed the siege and the massacre, in which 11 Israeli athletes and officials were killed by Black September, the global recriminations, and the launch of an Israeli revenge mission. The accompanying documentary film of the same name won the Academy Award for Documentary Feature and was screened in cinemas around the world. The book was described by *The New Yorker* as 'highly skilled and detailed...it's a page-turner'.

After the attacks of 9/11 Reeve began making travel documentaries for the BBC in obscure and troubled parts of the world. Tom Hall, Travel Editor, Lonely Planet publications, has described Reeve's travel documentaries as: "the best travel television programmes of the past five years". After vomiting blood and being diagnosed with malaria on a journey around the equator, Reeve became an ambassador for the Malaria Awareness Campaign.

Simon Reeve is the older brother of award-winning photographer James Reeve , former winner of the Nikon/ *Wanderlust/The Independent* International Professional Travel Photographer of the Year Award , who has been recognised by the National Portrait Gallery Portrait Prize and *the Observer* Hodge award for his work in Afghanistan.

BEN ANDERSON (JOURNALIST)

He is a television reporter and writer. He was born in Middlesbrough, and now lives in London. A veteran reporter and presenter, in 2005, Ben Anderson reported for *Frontline Football* – four films for the BBC that followed national football teams beset by turmoil during the qualifying rounds of the World Cup. In the previous year, he was a reporter on *Holidays in the Danger Zone* - The Violent Coast. This four part series for BBC2 focused on travelling along West Africa's notoriously dangerous coast. Back in 2003, Ben was a reporter on *Correspondent - Terror in South East Asia*, which profiled Khalid Sheikh Mohammed's time in Manila with Ramsi Yousef, prior to the September 11 attacks.

Anderson is perhaps most famous for *Holidays in the Axis of Evil*, the BBC series where he travelled secretly to Iran, Iraq, North Korea, Syria, Libya and Cuba. He also made films about gang wars in El Salvador, the landless movement in Brazil, pollution in Varanasi, Maoist insurgents in Bihar, water rights for Palestinians in the West Bank, the third generation of Agent Orange victims in Vietnam, deportees and pimps in Cambodia and the war in Southern Iraq. Ben is also the presenter of *World's Toughest Tribes* – a six part television documentary series for Discovery Channel that focuses on unique modern day tribes.

His recent work included "Taking on the Taliban", a harrowing film that resulted from two months in Helmand, Afghanistan's most violent province, with the Queen's Company, Grenadier Guards. The film was shortlisted for RTS programme and Journalism awards, as a well as a BAFTA. His diary from Helmand was published by the London review of Books.

He has since covered Slave labour in Dubai, and new threats and solutions to deforestation for BBC 1's Panorama. He has been back to Helmand several times, for Newsnight, the Times, the Guardian magazine, GQ and VBS (where Spike Jonze singled out his film "Obama's War" as amongst the best of 2009.)

M.I.A. wrote a hit single about Ben Anderson, and he has worked with World Champion David Hayemaker Haye on a film.

MARK CARWARDINE

Mark Carwardine (born 9 March 1959) is a zoologist who achieved widespread recognition for his *Last Chance to See* conservation expeditions with Douglas Adams, first aired on BBC Radio 4 in 1990. Since then he has become a leading conservationist and a prolific broadcaster, columnist and photographer.

Carwardine has written more than 50 books. Most recently he has written *Last Chance to See: In the Footsteps of Douglas Adams* (HarperCollins, 2009). This is a sequel to the best-selling book, *Last Chance to See,* which he wrote with the late Douglas Adams (author of *The Hitchhiker's Guide to the Galaxy*). Other books that Carwardine has written include the award-winning *Shark Watcher's Handbook* and *Eyewitness Handbooks: Whales, Dolphins and Porpoises,* which is the best-selling cetacean field guide ever published (nearly a million copies in print). Carwardine also writes a monthly column in *BBC Wildlife* magazine, and has written hundreds of articles for newspapers and magazines.

Radio and Television

Carwardine most recently co-presented *Stephen Fry and the Great American Oil Slick* (BBC2, 7 November 2010). In spring 2010, he co-presented *The Museum of Life*(BBC2, 6 episodes), which explored the pioneering and often surprising research work and wildlife collections of the Natural History Museum, in London. In autumn 2009, he joined forces with Stephen Fry to present a six-part BBC2 television series, *Last Chance to See* about endangered species – as inspired by the best-selling book of the same name, which Carwardine wrote some 20 years ago with the late Douglas Adams.

The TV series updated most of the endangered species featured in the original book and looked at many other new ones, including the Amazonian manatee, the northern white rhino in the Democratic Republic of the Congo, the aye-aye in Madagascar, the Komodo dragon in Indonesia, the kakapo in

New Zealand and the blue whale in Baja California, Mexico. There was an update about the elusive northern white rhino's plight, *Last Chance to See: Return of the Rhino* (BBC2, October 2010).

The original book (1990) and subsequent Radio 4 series described eight expeditions to find endangered species around the world: the aye-aye in Madagascar, Komodo dragon in Indonesia, kakapo in New Zealand, Amazonian manatee in Brazil, Yangtze river dolphin in China, Juan Fernandez fur seal in Chile, northern white rhino in the Democratic Republic of the Congo and Rodrigues fruit bat in Mauritius.

Carwardine also presented the weekly half-hour radio programme Nature, on BBC Radio 4, for many years. He has also been the presenter of many other programmes for BBC Radio 4.

Carwardine has an extensive collection of wildlife, nature and environment photographs taken on all seven continents and in more than a hundred countries. Since 2005, he has also been Chairman of the judging panel for the prestigious Wildlife Photographer of the Year competition, run by the Natural History Museum and *BBC Wildlife*.

Carwardine was a founding director of the wildlife travel companies Discover the World, WildOceans and Ocean Wanderers, and now runs whale-watching tours to Baja California, Mexico and occasional specialist wildlife photography trips.

Carwardine has recently started a wildlife illustration agency, the Wildlife Art Company, which sells natural-history illustrations to publishers.

Earls Court

Earl's Court is a district in the Royal Borough of Kensington and Chelsea in London, England. It is an inner-city district centred on Earl's Court Road and surrounding streets, located 3.1 miles (5 km) west south-west of Charing Cross. It borders the sub-districts of South Kensington to the East, West

Kensington to the West, Chelsea to the South and Kensington to the North. The Earls Court ward had a population of 9,659 according to the 2001 Census.It is home to the Earls Court Exhibition Centre, one of the country's largest indoor arenas and a popular concert venue.

Earls Court was once a rural area, covered with green fields and market gardens. The Saxon Thegn Edwin held the lordship of the area prior to the Norman Conquest. For over 500 years the land, part of the ancient manor of Kensington, was under the lordship of the Vere family, the Earls of Oxford and descendants of Aubrey de Vere I, who held the manor of Geoffrey de Montbray, bishop of Coutances, in Domesday Book in 1086. By *circa* 1095, his tenure had been converted, and he held Kensington directly of the crown. A church had been constructed there by 1104. The earls held their manorial court where Old Manor Yard is now, just by the London Underground station. Earls Court Farm is visible on Greenwood's map of London dated 1827.

Railway Line

The construction of the Metropolitan District Railway station in 1865–69 was a catalyst for development. In the quarter century after 1867, Earls Court was transformed into a densely populated suburb with 1,200 houses and two churches. Eardley Crescent and Kempsford Gardens were built between 1867 and 1873, building began in Earls Court Square and Longridge Road in 1873, in Nevern Place in 1874, in Trebovir Road and Philbeach Gardens in 1876, and Nevern Square in 1880.

Population

Following WWII a number of Polish immigrants settled in the Earls Court area leading to Earls Court Road being dubbed 'The Danzig Corridor'. During the late 1960s a large transient population of Australia and New Zealand travellers began to use Earls Court as a UK hub and over time it gained the name 'Kangaroo Valley'. It was at the time one of the cheapest areas close to central London, and up until the 1990s remained a somewhat down-at-heel district compared to its more upmarket neighbours to the North and East. The area was, for along time, the place to buy and sell the ubiquitous VW camper van. This moved off in the direction of the New North Road (near Old St EC1) in the 1980's.

Today, while there are still significant numbers of students or other people on temporary visas, many of the Australians and New Zealanders appear to have moved on to now-cheaper areas further North and West. The name "Kangaroo Valley" lingers on in the usage of older ex-patriate Australians and Australian visitors, as does the alternative nickname "Kangaroo Court".

The change in the area's population is largely owed to rocketing property prices and the continued gentrification of the area. The scale of change is illustrated by the economic divide between the eastern and western areas of Earl's Court.

Notable people

Blue Plaques in Earls Court

- Howard Carter (1874–1939), English archaeologist, Egyptologist and primary discoverer of the tomb of Tutankhamun, lived at 19 Collingham Gardens.
- Benjamin Britten (1913–1976), English composer, conductor, violist and pianist, lived at 173 Cromwell Road.
- Edwin Arnold (1832–1904), English poet and journalist, lived at 31 Bolton Gardens.
- Alfred Hitchcock (1899–1980), English filmmaker and producer, lived at 153 Cromwell Road.
- Edmund Allenby, 1st Viscount Allenby (1861–1936), British soldier and administrator famous for his role during World War I when he led the Egyptian Expeditionary Force in the conquest of Palestine and Syria, lived at 24 Wetherby Gardens.
- Dame Ellen Terry (1847–1928), leading Shakespearian stage actress in Britain in the 1880s and 1890s, lived at 22 Barkston Gardens.

- Sir William Orpen (1878–1931), Irish portrait painter, lived at 8 South Bolton Gardens.
- Norman Lockyer (1836–1920), English scientist and astronomer credited with discovering the gas helium, lived at 16 Penywern Road.

Other Notable Residents

- Diana, Princess of Wales (1961–1997), the first wife of Charles, Prince of Wales, lived at 60 Coleherne Court, Old Brompton Road, from 1979 - 1981. The 3-bedroom flat was bought for her by her parents for £50,000 as an 18th birthday present. Diana, who shared the space with three room-mates who paid her £18 per week rent, once said it was where she spent the happiest time of her life. Diana lived there until February 1981 when she moved into Clarence House, the Queen Mother's residence, on the night before her engagement to Prince Charles was officially announced. In the 1990s, Diana regularly returned to the area to work out at Earls Court Gym (now part of the Soho Gyms chain) next to Earls Court underground station.
- Freddie Mercury (1946-91), flamboyant lead singer with the world-renowned rock group Queen, lived, and died, at a house at 1 Logan Place, just off the Earls Court Road
- Stewart Granger (1913–1993), Hollywood actor, was born in Coleherne Court, Old Brompton Road, and spent most of his childhood there.
- Horace Donisthorpe (1870–1951), British myrmecologist and coleopterist, lived at 58 Kensington Mansions, Trebovir Road. Memorable for championing the renaming of the genus Lasius after him as Donisthorpea, and for discovering new species of beetles and ants, he is often considered the greatest figure in British myrmecology.
- Major Sir William Palliser (1830–1882), Irish-born politician and inventor, Member of Parliament for

Taunton from 1880 to his death, lived in Earls Court Square.

- Gary Barlow (1971), English singer, has a home in Earls Court.
- H. G. Pelissier (1874–1913), English theatrical producer, composer and satirist, lived at 1 Nevern Square
- Howard Spensley (1834–1902), Australian lawyer and British Liberal politician, lived in Earls Court Square.

FILM LOCATIONS

Kensington Mansions, on the north side of Trebovir Road, was the mysterious mansion block in Roman Polanski's movie Repulsion (1965), in which the sexually repressed Carole Ledoux (played by Catherine Deneuve) has a murderous breakdown. The film won the Silver Berlin Bear-Extraordinary Jury Prize at the Berlin Film Festival later the same year.

64 Redcliffe Square is featured in An American Werewolf in London (1981). The movie is a horror/comedy about two American tourists in London who are attacked by a werewolf that none of the locals admit exists. The flat in the Square belongs to Alex (Jenny Agutter), a pretty young nurse who becomes infatuated with one of the two American college students (David Kessler).

LOCAL ATTRACTIONS

Earls Court is within easy walking distance of High Street Kensington, Holland Park, Kensington Gardens/Hyde Park, the Royal Albert Hall, Imperial College, the Natural History, Science and Victoria and Albert Museums.

The largest draw for visitors to Earls Court is its Exhibition Centre, opened in the present building in 1937, with its striking Art Deco facade facing Warwick Road. A new entrance to Earl's Court tube station was constructed to facilitate easy access to the Exhibition Centre, including direct entrance from the underground passage which connects the District and Piccadilly lines. This was however closed in the 1990s at around the time the capacity of the Exhibition Centre was expanded by the construction of a second exhibition hall, Earls Court 2, which was opened by Princess Diana, herself a former Earls Court resident.

In its heyday the Earls Court Exhibition Centre hosted many of the leading national trade fairs, including the annual Motor Show and Royal Agricultural Show, as well as Crufts dog show and the military Royal Tournament. The biggest trade fairs migrated to the National Exhibition Centre at Birmingham International Airport when it opened in 1988. The longest-running annual show is now the Ideal Home Show in April, which still attracts tens of thousands of visitors.

Otherwise, it has increasingly been used as a live music venue, hosting events such as the farewell concert by then boy-band Take That. At the other end of the scale, it has been used for arena-style opera performances of Carmen and Aida. Archive Movietone newsreel footage (which can be seen on YouTube) captures a unique and powerful rehearsal of the Berlin Philharmonic Orchestra under Wilhelm Furtwängler playing the end of Brahms' Fourth Symphony during a post-War reconciliation visit to London.

Capital and Counties - the owners of the Earls Court Exhibition Centre - have the intention of closing the venue, and it is expected that the site will be redeveloped by 2020 with a mixture of office and residential buildings.

A further landmark building is the Empress State Building, located in Lillie Road, which was completed in 1962, and is a unique triangular office building with concave bow facades. It was occupied by the Ministry of Defence for 30 years. It underwent extensive refurbishment and updating prior to its occupation by the Metropolitan Police around 2003.

The multi-award-winning Finborough Theatre, which opened in 1980, is the neighbourhood's local theatre.

The Troubadouris a coffee house and a small music venue,

which has hosted emerging talent since 1954 - including Bob Dylan, Jimi Hendrix and Elvis Costello. In 2009 Les Routiers UK gave The Troubadour their Best UK Cafe Award.

Earls Court Village is the centre of the Filipino British community, where it has a number of Asian restaurants, Filipino supermarkets (many of which also serve take-away food), and Filipino banks.

The area is also home to the UK's only real-life "TARDIS", so called because it resembles Dr Who's time machine in the BBC television series. The blue police box located outside Earls Court underground station in Earls Court Road is actually a modern day replica of the traditional GPO police signalboxes that were once a common sight in the UK until the early 1970s. Used as a kind of specialised telephone kiosk for policemen on their "beat", the boxes were eventually phased out with the introduction of personal radios in the police force.

NEIGHBOURHOODS

East Earls Court

"East Earls Court" lies to the south of Cromwell Road and to the east of Earl's Court Road (a main North-South artery and now the Western Boundary of the London Congestion Charge which bisects Earls Court) and is home to many multi-million-pound apartments and houses in smart garden squares and residential streets. The southern boundary of Earls Court is Old Brompton Road, with the area to the south being West Brompton, and the area to the south east being The Beach Area of Chelsea. Here, (based on sale prices per square foot), The Boltons, has some of the most costly real estate in Europe. Houses in The Boltons' have sold for up to £20 million. The eastern boundary of Earls Court is Collingham Road, east of which is South Kensington.

West Earls Court

"West Earls Court," lying to the west of Earls Court Road, is notably different in architecture. White stucco fronted "boutique" hotels in Trebovir Road and Templeton Place, and the impressive late-Victorian mansion flats and town houses of Earls Court Square, Nevern Square and Kensington Mansions, contrast with the area's remaining cheaper hotels and apartment houses full of bedsits (also known as bed-sitters or bed-sitting rooms).

There are some impressive examples of early- to mid-Victorian architecture in the Earls Court ward. Gardens such as Bramham Gardens and Courtfield Gardens are beautiful traditional residential squares with many imposing properties fronting onto them and in the case of Courtfield Gardens, traditional cast iron railings around the enclosed gardens have just been restored (the originals having been removed in 1940 for scrap iron during World War 2) creating a more authentic Victorian ambience.

Further west, Kensington Mansions, Nevern Square and Philbeach Gardens are built around impressive formal garden settings (access limited to key holding residents). Collingham Road and Harrington Road, also have some unique buildings, many of them very large and currently used as Embassies.

A little further north, just south of the Cromwell Road, the tranquil conservation area comprising Childs Place, Kenway Road, Wallgrave Road and Redfield Lane contains fine examples of more modest terraced townhouses painted in pastel shades in a very picturesque setting with some fine floral displays. Hidden in the middle of this area is London's smallest communal garden, "Providence Patch" built on the site of former stables serving the surrounding houses, which were destroyed by a bomb in 1941. A glimpse of the (private) gardens can be seen via the original stable entrance way in Wallgrave Road

CENTRE OF GAY NIGHTLIFE

Earls Court preceded Soho as London's centre of gay nightlife, though the number of businesses aimed mostly at gay men has dwindled to a couple of retail outlets, as Soho and Vauxhall established themselves as the focus of gay nightlife. The first public nightclub aimed at a gay clientele, The Copacabana, opened in Earls Court Road in the late 1970's, but was re-themed as a general venue in the late 1990s. The bar upstairs, Harpies and Louies, was until the late 1980s the most popular gay bar in London. It is now the Wagamama restaurant.

In 1964, The Lord Ranelagh Pub (opposite the former Princess Beatrice Hospital) spearheaded the local demand for live entertainment. A young, non-gay, male band, The Downtowners, attracted considerable attention. They persuaded many of the local cross-dressers to come into the pub and perform. Thus, the Queen of the Month contest was born. Every Saturday night the pub was packed to capacity.

The show ran from September 1964 until May 1965 when the News of the World ran an article entitled 'This show must not go on.' On that Sunday night the pub was so packed that every table and chair had to be removed. Crowds spilled out on to the pavement onto Old Brompton Road. The police closed the show. Many well known celebrities were among the clientele and the Lord Ranelagh is considered to have played a role in the history of gay liberation. The pub underwent several different incarnations as a gay nightclub, the last as "Infinity", but is now closed.

The Pembroke pub, formerly the Coleherne, dates from the 1880s and had a long history of attracting a bohemian clientele before becoming known as a gay pub. A life-long resident of Earls Court Square, Jennifer Ware, recollects as a child being taken there to Sunday lunch in the 1930's, when drag entertainers performed after lunch had finished. In the 1970s it became a notorious Leather bar, with blacked-out windows, attracting an international crowd including the likes of Freddie Mercury, Kenny Everett and Rudolf Nureyev.

It also became infamous as the stalking ground for three separate serial killers from the 1970s to the 1990s: Dennis Nilsen, Michael Lupo and Colin Ireland. It sought to lighten its image with a makeover in the mid-1990s to attract a wider clientele; to no avail, as in December 2008 it underwent a major refurbishment and repositioned itself as a gastro pub with a new name.

Earls Court Exhibition Centre

The Earls Court Exhibition Centre is an exhibition centre, conference and event venue located in west London, England in the Royal Borough of Kensington and Chelsea . It is the largest exhibition venue in central London. It is served by two underground stations, Earl's Court and West Brompton, opposite its entrances on Warwick Road and the Old Brompton Road. Earls Court and nearby Olympia are operated by EC&O Venues.

Earls Court was largely a waste ground for many years. With the introduction of two stations, it became a mass network of rail on derelict grounds. The idea of introducing entertainment to the grounds was brought about by an entrepreneur called John Robinson Whitley who used the land as a show ground for many years. Whitley did not profit from his efforts, yet his desire had decided the future of Earls Court and its purpose in later years. In the late 19th century the site had been home to Buffalo Bill's Wild West Show and a huge observation wheel. A plaque in the press centre commemorates both of these facts and that Queen Victoria was a frequent visitor to the show.

In 1935, the land was sold and the new owners decided to construct a show centre to rival any other in the world and to dominate the nearby Olympia exhibition hall. The plan was to create Europe's largest structure by volume. The project did not go exactly to plan; it ran over budget and was late in completion. Earls Court finally opened its door to the public for the Chocolate and Confectionery Exhibition on 1 September 1937.

It was designed by architect C. Howard Crane. The Motor Show and Commercial Vehicle show soon followed. In spite of all the problems in the latter part of construction, the project was completed at a cost of £1.5 million. This building is now usually referred to as Earls Court One. It has 41,811 square metres of space on two levels.

Earls Court Two

In response to the drastic need to increase Earls Court's exhibition space, Earls Court Two was constructed at a cost of £100m. The striking new barrel-roofed hall which links with Earls Court One via folding shutters is large enough to hold four Boeing 747's (jumbo jets), and the hall's 17,000 square metre floor is entirely column-free. The hall was opened by Diana, Princess of Wales on 17 October 1991 for the Motorfair. Earls Court 2 is situated on part of the former Lillie Bridge.

Redevelopment Plans

The owners of Earls Court and Olympia are Capital and Counties. They are presently in discussion with the boroughs of Hammersmith and Fulham and the Royal Borough of Kensington and Chelsea to demolish the existing centre and redevelop the area with up to 8000 new flats, retail and possibly a new convention centre. However this is expected to take many years work and certainly can't commence until after the Olympics in 2012.

3

INTERNATIONAL HOSPITALITY FAIR IN USA

You don't want to miss the most important Travel & Tourism trade events. We identify the top shows, and then we work with the organizers to provide special added value - such as US Pavilions - for U.S. companies that participate. Commercial Service staff attend the shows, and often provide matchmaking services for U.S. companies. U.S. shows that are part of the Department of Commerce's International Buyer Program will feature overseas delegations and an International Business Center staffed by Department of Commerce employees.

VISIT USA WORKSHOP

TBD 2011

The Workshop organized by Visit USA in cooperation with Commercial Service is held annually just before ITB Berlin. It is known to be the best event for US travel professionals in Belgium. It gives a unique opportunity to promote USA tourism regions, products and services to the Belgium and Luxembourg markets. The workshop is exclusively open to travel agents and press. The 2008 Workshop showcased 45 exhibiting organizations and was attended by over 200 travel agents and 15 travel journalists. Both exhibitors and visitors commented on the 2008 Workshop.

Hospitality Design Exposition & Conference

May 18 - 20, 2011

May 17, 2011, Green Day

Sands Expo & Convention Center

Las Vegas, Nevada

The Center of Design and Innovation

The Hospitality Design (HD) Exposition & Conference is the premier trade show for the hospitality industry established in 1992. It is THE essential show of the year for professionals interested in opportunities to learn, grow and connect with other businesses in this dynamic field. The HD Expo has the largest collection of hospitality related exhibitors in the country.

- **More than 900 exhibitors**: Manufacturers and artisans from around the world gather together under one roof on one level offering their latest and best inventions and ideas.
- LU/CEU accredited, **peer-based conference sessions and key-note speakers** provide insight into trends and market forces that shape the hospitality industry.
- Invaluable **networking events** build and solidify relationships with trade leaders and fellow associates.

Florida Restaurant & Lodging Show

More than a trade show, the **Florida Restaurant & Lodging Show** is a complete learning experience that improves your business throughout. From new products, to new tricks of the trade, to gold-standard food service education, you'll gain real-world solutions you can apply to your business immediately.

Don't miss your opportunity to participate in next year's event...please check back for more information on the 2011 show.

National Restaurant Association - NRA Show

For all you long-lead planners, NRA Show 2011 is set for May 21-24, 2011 in Chicago at McCormick Place.

Only NRA Show 2010 offers the wide breadth and depth of information that you can immediately take home and put to work. Over 65 FREE education sessions and non-stop culinary demonstrations cover food trends, cost savings, gluten-free menu development, guest acquisition & retention, "going green," employee recruitment and many other topics that are vital to growing your top- and bottom-line results. On the Show floor, test products from over 1,500 exhibitors in 950 product categories, all under one roof:

- beverage
- educational
- equipment
- food
- furnishings & decorations
- furniture
- linens
- lodging
- paper, plastics & supplies
- services
- tableware
- technology
- uniforms

Los Angeles Times Travel & Adventure Show

At the Los Angles Convention Center! It's the largest travel event in the U.S.! Get Show Only specials and giveaways on travel you won't find anywhere else! See the complete list of specials you'll only find at the Travel & Adventure Show!

From safaris to scuba diving, wind surfing to wine tours, archeology excursions to relaxing on a pristine beach, here's where you'll discover amazing travel destinations, attractions, activities, resorts, products, luxury goods and services and so much more! More than 500 exhibitors. Trip giveaways. Cultural entertainment. And travel experts Rick Steves, Arthur and Pauline Frommer and more. It's everything you need to get far away from the every day.

Opening Hours:

Travel Trade: Saturday 8 – 10 am

Public: Saturday & Sunday 10 am – 5 p

Anaheim, CA

City/Location	*Exhibition Name*	*Cycle*	*Naxt Date*
Anaheim Convention Center	Natural Products EXPO WEST Natural and Organic Industry Expo	once a year	10.03 - 13.03-2011
Anaheim, CA	IDDBA Dairy, Deli, Bakery, Cheese, Foodservice Products Seminar & Expo		05.06 - 07.06 2011
Hilton Anaheim	NUTRACON Conference on Product Innovation and Successful Brand Management for the Health and Nutrition Industry		09.03 - 11.03 2011

Baltimore, MD

City/Location	*Exhibition Name*	*Cycle*	*Naxt Date*
Baltimore Convention Center	BIOFACH AMERICA World Organic Products Expo. Trade Show & Congress	once a year	22.09 - 24.09 2011
Baltimore Convention Center	NATURAL PRODUCTS EXPO EAST Natural and Organic Trade Show	once a year	21.09 - 24.09 2011

Boston Convention & Exhibition Center	INTERNATIONAL BOSTON SEAFOOD SHOW International Sea Food Show	once a year	20.03 - 22.03 2011
Boston Convention & Exhibition Center	NEW ENGLAND FOOD SERVICE & LODGING EXPO Northeast Food Service & Lodging Expo	once a year	20.03 - 22.03 2011
Boston Convention & Exhibition Center	SEAFOOD PROCESSING AMERICA Sea Food Show	once a year	20.03 - 22.03 22.03 2011
Seaport World Trade Center	BOSTON WINE EXPO Wine Fair	once a year	Jan. 2012 (?)

Chicago, IL

City/Location	*Exhibition Name*	*Cycle*	*Naxt Date*
Embassy Suites Downtown	WORLD WINE MEETINGS AMERICA A Convention for Wines and Spirits from all over the World	once a year	29.04 - 01.05 2011
McCormick Place	ALL CANDY EXPO Candy Expo	once a year	24.05 - 26.05 2011
McCormick Place	ALL THINGS ORGANIC Business-to-Business Event Focusing exclusively on Organic Products	once a year	June 2011 (?)

Chicago, IL

City/Location	*Exhibition Name*	*Cycle*	*Naxt Date*
Embassy Suites Downtown	WORLD WINE MEETINGS AMERICA A Convention for Wines and Spirits from all over the World	once a year	29.04 - 01.05 2011

McCormick Place	ALL CANDY EXPO Candy Expo	once a year	24.05 - 26.05 2011
McCormick Place	ALL THINGS ORGANIC Business-to-Business Event Focusing exclusively on Organic Products	once a year	June 2011 (?)

Las Vegas, NV

City/Location	*Exhibition Name*	*Cycle*	*Naxt Date*
Las Vegas Convention Center	CATERSOURCE CONFERENCE & TRADESHOW Expo & Conference for owners, executive chefs and managers, food and beverage directors, culinary and sales staff	once a year	Feb. 2012 (?)
Las Vegas Convention Center	IBIE International Baking Industry Exposition	every 3 years	Sept. 2013 (?)
Las Vegas Convention Center	INTERNATIONAL PIZZA EXPO International Pizza Expo	once a year	March 2012 (?)
Las Vegas Convention Center	NIGHTCLUB & BAR - BEVERAGE AND FOOD SHOW International Nightclub & Bar/Beverage Retailer/ Beverage & Food Convention and Trade Show	once a year	07.03 - 09.03 2011

Los Angeles, CA

City/Location	*Exhibition Name*	*Cycle*	*Naxt Date*
Los Angeles Convention Center	EXPO COMIDA LATINA - LOS ANGELES Hispanic Food & Beverage Show	every 2 years	Aug. 2012 (?)

Miami, FL

City/Location	*Exhibition Name*	*Cycle*	*Naxt Date*
Miami Beach Convention Center	MIAMI INTERNATIONAL WINE FAIR Miami International Wine Fair	once a year	23.09 - 25.10 2011

New Orleans, LA

City/Location	*Exhibition Name*	*Cycle*	*Naxt Date*
Ernest N. Morial Convention Center	IFT ANNUAL MEETING & FOOD EXPO International Event for Food Science Professionals	once a year	11.06 - 15.06 2011

New York, NY

City/Location	*Exhibition Name*	*Cycle*	*Naxt Date*
Altman Building & Metropolitan Pavilion	CHOCOLATE SHOW - NEW YORK chocolate Show	once a year	Nov. 2011 (?)
Jacob K. Javits Convention Center	INTERNATIONAL HOTEL / MOTEL & RESTAURANT SHOW Premier Trade Event for the Hospitality Industry	once a year	12.11 - 15.11 2011
Jacob K. Javits Convention Center	INTERNATIONAL RESTAURANT & FOODSERVICE SHOW OF NEW YORK The show delivers the critical trends, latest cost-saving products and services, state-of-the-art equipment and never-before-tasted foods. Including such areas as the International Tasting Arena, Three Demo Cooking Theaters, Hispanic Foods Expo...	once a year	Feb. 2012 (?)

Jacob K. Javits Convention Center	NEW YORK WINE EXPO Wine Fair	once a year	Feb. 2012 (?)

Orlando, FL

City/Location	*Exhibition Name*	*Cycle*	*Naxt Date*
Orange County Convention Center	FLORIDA RESTAURANT & LODGING SHOW Florida Foodservice Industry Trade Show	once a year	08.09 - 10.09 2011

Palm Beach, FL

City/Location	*Exhibition Name*	*Cycle*	*Naxt Date*
Palm Beach, FL	FA&M Food Engineering's Food Automation & Manufacturing Conference and Expo	once a year	03.04 - 06.04 2011

Sacramento, CA

City/Location	*Exhibition Name*	*Cycle*	*Naxt Date*
Sacramento Convention Center	UNIFIED WINE & GRAPE SYMPOSIUM The largest wine and grape conference & expo in the USA	once a year	24.01 - 26.01 2012

San Diego, CA

City/Location	*Exhibition Name*	*Cycle*	*Naxt Date*
San Diego Convention Center	EXPO COMIDA LATINA - SAN DIEGO Hispanic Food & Beverage Show	unknown	28.08 - 30.08 2011
San Diego Convention Center	WESTERN FOODSERVICE & HOSPITALITY EXPO Western Food Service & Hospitality Expo	once a year	28.08 - 30.08 2011

San Francisco, CA

City/Location	*Exhibition Name*	*Cycle*	*Naxt Date*
Moscone Convention Center	WINTER FANCY FOOD SHOW International Fancy Food & Confection Show	once a year	16.01 - 18.01 2011
San Francisco, CA	SAN FRANCISCO CASH & CARRY SHOW Gift and Collectibles, Gourmet Food Products, Fine & Fashion Jewelry, Bath and Spa Items, Aromatherapy as well as Handcrafted Items, Personal & Fashion Accessories and Antiques and Found Objects	once a year	Oct. 2011 (?)
San Francisco, CA	WORLD ALGAE CONGRESS USA International Algae Congress	unknown	06.12 - 08.12 2010

Seattle, WA

City/Location	*Exhibition Name*	*Cycle*	*Naxt Date*
Qwest Field and Event Center	PACIFIC MARINE EXPO West Coast Trade Show for the Commercial Fishing, Seafood Processing, and Workboat Markets	once a year	Nov. 2011 (?)
Washington State Convention & Trade Center	SEATTLE CASH & CARRY SHOW Gift and Collectibles, Gourmet Food Products, Fine & Fashion Jewelry, Bath and Spa Items, Aromatherapy as well as Handcrafted Items, Personal & Fashion Accessories and Antiques and Found Objects	once a year	Nov. 2011 (?)

Vancouver, WA

City/Location	*Exhibition Name*	*Cycle*	*Naxt Date*
Esther Short Park	VANCOUVER WINE & JAZZ FESTIVAL International Wine & Jazz Festival	once a year	26.08 - 28.08 2011

Washington D.C.

City/Location	*Exhibition Name*	*Cycle*	*Naxt Date*
Ronald Reagan Building and International Trade Center	WASHINGTON D.C. INTER-NATIONAL WINE & FOOD FESTIVAL Washington D.C. International Wine & Food Festival	once a year	Feb. 2012 (?)
Washington D.C.	SUMMER FANCY FOOD SHOW International Fancy Food & Confection Show	once a year	10.07 - 12.07 2011

FOOD FAIR

Food Fair, also known by its successor name Pantry Pride, was a large supermarket chain in the United States. It was founded by Samuel N. Friedland, who opened the first store (as Reading Giant Quality Price Cutter) in Harrisburg, Pennsylvania in the late 1920s. As of 1957, Food Fair had 275 stores, and at its peak, the chain had more than 500 stores. Friedland's family retained control of the firm through 1978, when the chain entered bankruptcy.

Origins

Samuel Friedland opened his first "Reading Giant Quality Price Cutter" supermarket in the 1920s. The success of the first store led to the opening of more stores, and by the late 1940s, and the introduction of a new name: Food Fair.

In 1958, Food Fair purchased Setzer's Supermarkets, a 40-store Jacksonville, Florida chain. In 1961, the company bought J.M. Fields Department Stores, a chain of discount department stores in New England.

The latter chain grew substantially, expanding the stores to areas already served by Food Fair, particularly Florida. By the 1960s, most J.M. Fields stores featured a J.M. Fields or Food Fair/Pantry Pride grocery store.

The Birth of Pantry Pride

During the 1960s, Food Fair enjoyed great success, but the most significant purchase for the company was that of a small Philadelphia chain called Best Markets. Best's private label brand was called Pantry Pride. When the company launched a chain of no-frills discount grocery stores in mid-decade, they used the name "Pantry Pride".

The stores that were under the "Pantry Pride" logo eventually became so popular, they eclipsed the "Food Fair" brand as the company's dominant trademark banner. By 1970, Food Fair had converted most of its stores to the Pantry Pride banner, and the company began to rise to new heights.

Expansion in the 1960s and 1970s

In the late 1960s, the company, led by its Pantry Pride stores, continued to grow. The company also opened additional J.M. Fields stores and entered new businesses, launching drug stores, gasoline stations and shoe stores. It also boosted its core business by entering the California and Nevada markets through the purchase of the Fox Markets chain. The western expansion proved exhausting for the predominantly East Coast retailer, and it eventually divested itself of the 50 stores by 1972. In 1976 it acquired Hills Supermarkets of New York. Later that year it purchased the remaining 17 stores from the Philadelphia-based Penn Fruit Company.

Slow Decline, 1978-2000

In 1978, Food Fair fell victim to financial problems. It entered bankruptcy that year and a new management team, led by supermarket veteran Grant Gentry, began streamlining the 456-store $2.7 billion dollar company. By the end of 1978 the company took the first steps in the long journey out of bankruptcy by closing all of the JM Fields stores. Those stores were quickly purchased by Caldor, Jefferson Ward and Kmart.

In early 1979, the company left its home market of Philadelphia, where the firm was headquartered, closing its more than 50 stores in the area, even though it was the second largest chain in greater Philadelphia in terms of market share. Between 1979 and 1981, more than 200 stores were closed, along with several warehouses. Food-a-Rama bought 14 of its 48 Baltimore-area stores in 1981. By this time, Food Fair had emerged from bankruptcy, and was based in Fort Lauderdale, Florida under the name Pantry Pride Stores, Inc.

The company had entered into talks to be purchased by Pathmark Stores that same year, but discussions were abandoned when Pantry Pride's stockholders filed a complaint. Pantry Pride outsourced its wholesale operations to Supervalu when it sold its Miami and Jacksonville distribution centers. The company then began selling off huge chunks of its assets when it sold two-thirds of its remaining stores, including the last of its Richmond, Virginia stores to A&P. Only about 40 stores in southern Florida remained.

In 1984, in separate transactions, Pantry Pride acquired Devon Stores, a home improvement store and the 400-store Adams Drug Company, which operated in the northeastern United States. The owner of Devon Stores, who obtained about 10.4% of the merged company, then sought an ouster of the Pantry Pride Board of Directors. In 1985, using junk bonds, 38% of Pantry Pride was acquired by investor Ronald Perelman. This was enough to acquire control, and Perelman liquidated its assets but kept its losses on the books to offset profits from MacAndrews and Forbes, which he had previously acquired. Perelman used Pantry Pride as a vehicle to acquire other companies, in particular Revlon. By 1986, the name of Pantry Pride was changed to Revlon Group.

In 1985, the last stores in southern Florida were sold to Red Apple Group, a New York supermarket chain owned by John Catsimadidis. By 1990, the chain was being supplied by the Fleming Companies. The last store opened in 1991 in Sunny Isles, Florida. By this time, nearly all of the stores were renamed Wooley's, after acquiring the latter named chain of seven stores in the early 1990s. In 1993, Fleming bought the Wooley's chain after a dispute with Catsimadidis. The remaining stores were either closed or sold by 2000.

Timeline

- 1920s - Food Fair Stores founded by Russian immigrant Samuel N. Friedland in Harrisburg, Pennsylvania.
- 1957 - Food Fair has 275 stores.
- 1958 - Food Fair purchases 40-store Jacksonville, Florida based Setzer's Supermarkets.
- 1965 - Acquires J.M. Fields Department Stores.
- mid-1960s - Acquires Best Markets and Pantry Pride private label brand, launches Pantry Pride branded discount supermarkets soon after
- 1967(?)- Purchases Fox Supermarkets in California and Nevada.
- 1972(?)- Divests Fox Supermarkets
- 1976 - Purchased Hills Supermarkets (NY)
- 1976 - Remaining 17 of bankrupt Penn Fruit's Philadelphia area stores are acquired by Food Fair.
- 1978 - Enters Chapter 11 Bankruptcy Protection. Friedland family gives up control of the company.
- 1981 - Exits Chapter 11 bankruptcy, re-organizes with new corporate name: Pantry Pride Stores, Inc., and moves company headquarters to Fort Lauderdale, FL.
- 1983-84 Sells last two distribution centers to Supervalu, who in turn sold them to Malone and Hyde and Winn-Dixie.

- 1984 - Pantry Pride operates 122 supermarkets in Florida, southern Georgia, the Tidewater region of Virginia, and the Bahamas.
- 1984 - Purchases Rhode Island based Adams/Brooks Drug Stores (approx. 400 drug stores in the northeast, principally in New England).
- 1984 - Purchases Devon Stores Corp., a 61-store home center chain with locations near U.S. military bases. Sells Virginia division to A&P.
- 1985 - Acquires Revlon Corp. as a holding company in Ronald Perelman's hostile takeover bid.
- 1985 - Samuel Friedland died at age 88 in Miami Beach, FL.
- 1986 - With only a handful of stores (southern Florida), Pantry Pride sells its remaining stores to Gristedes Supermarkets (NY) chairman John Catsimatidis. Now out of the retail grocery business, corporate name is changed to The Revlon Group, and moves corporate headquarters from Fort Lauderdale to New York.
- 1988 - Catsimatidis takes on Fleming Companies as a partner after Fleming purchases Malone & Hyde.
- 1991 - Last supermarket opened (Pantry Pride Food Emporium) in Sunny Isles, FL., most other stores are renamed Wooley's.
- 1993 - All remaining Pantry Pride/Wooley's Supermarkets are sold to Fleming.

OREGON COUNTRY FAIR

The Oregon Country Fair (OCF) is an annual three-day fair held in Veneta, Oregon, United States. Located in the Willamette Valley, the site is about 15 miles (24 km) west of Eugene along the Long Tom River. Annual attendance is approximately 45,000,and the fair has around 350 booths each year. The event is known as an outgrowth of the counter-culture movement, including an emphasis on using environmentally friendly practices during the fair. The Oregon Country Fair begins on the Friday of the second weekend in July every year.

The first fair was held in Eugene, on November 1 and November 2, 1969, and had as a tag-line, "come in costume". The fair began as a barter and craft fair to raise funds for an alternative school, the Children's Community School. The event moved to its current location in Veneta, about 14 miles west of Eugene, for the fall fair in October, 1970, after having had a May Fair the same year on Crow Road, about halfway between Eugene and Veneta.

In August 1972, the OCF site was used for the first of what was supposed to be a series of concerts held every ten years by the Grateful Dead. Known as "Field Trips", that first concert was held as a benefit for the Springfield Creamery, which is owned by members of Ken Kesey's family. Until 1977, the fair was known as the Oregon Renaissance Faire.

Entertainment

During open hours (11 am to 7 pm) there are 18 stages featuring a wide variety of musical, comedic, theatrical, juggling, daredevil, and vaudeville performances.

The stages are: Main Stage, Daredevil Palace, Shady Grove Stage, Kesey Stage, Gypsy Stage, W.C. Fields Stage, Spirit Tower, Rabbit Hole, Front Porch, Blue Moon Stage, Stage Left, Chez Ray's Next Stage, Monkey Palace, Might Tiny Puppet Stage, Hoarse Chorale, Morningwood Odditorium, Community Village, and Youth Stage.

Musical acts incorporate many styles, including: folk, rock, jazz, blues, bluegrass, Latin, slam poetry and spoken word. There are many path-side venues, parades, and walking performers throughout the entire fair site, including a marching band, giant puppets, and stilt walkers. There is also a drum circle at the Drum Tower which is open to all willing participants who bring their musical instruments.

Tickets and Transportation

Tickets and passes are required to attend the Oregon Country Fair. All tickets sold to the public are sold in advance at TicketsWest outlets and other retail centers throughout the Northwest. All tickets must be purchased off-site; no tickets will be sold at the fair site at any time. Discount tickets are available for people who qualify for disability or senior discounts.. There is no fee for children who are under the age of ten, and come with a paying adult. Public transportation, in the form of bus shuttle, is added in order to park and ride between Eugene and the OCF grounds non-stop throughout the days of the fair.

Culture

The fair is a family event with face painting, puppet shows, and music for children. Full nudity is not allowed during public hours in public areas—genitals must be covered at these times. No alcohol is allowed and smoking is limited to designated areas. The fair has its own water and communications systems, recycling service, emergency medical team, traffic control, and security team.

Infrastructure

The fair is a 501(c)(3) non-profit organization. It is governed by an elected twelve-member Board of Directors. There are seven staff positions within the organization.

Alter-Abled Access is available at the Oregon Country Fair, including: wheelchairs (there is a battery re-charging station for electric wheelchairs), helpers, sign language interpreters, folding chairs, rest areas, maps, and other information. To obtain these services, or more information about them, event participants can go to the following locations on the event site: the *Alter-Abled Access Advocates(4A)Center* (located near Admissions as well as at the Bus Stop), *Community Village, Solutions,* and all *Information booths.* From June 1 through August 31 there are no dogs allowed on the event site. The exception is for service dogs.

Publications

The Oregon Country Fair publishes a newsletter, the Fair Family News, eleven times a year. As well as an event paper, the Peach Pit, once a year for the three-day event.

Volunteer Crews

The Oregon Country Fair has a large volunteer network. This volunteer network is the base for all operational needs of the event. The different volunteer crews are:

Admissions, Advertising, Alter-Abled, Archaeology, Banners and Signs, Buses, Camping, Cart Central, Cartography, Childcare, Commemorative Sales, Community Village Council ,Communications, Construction, Craft Inventory, Crew Services, Entertainment Crew, Fair Family News, Fire Crew, Food Booth Committee ,General Store ,Green Thumb, Hospitality, Ice, Information, Kitchen Crews, Lot Crew, Main Camp, Medical, Office, Neighborhood Response Team, Peach Pit, Recycling, Registration, Sanitation, Security, Site Crew, Teen Crew, Traffic, Veg-man-ecs, Video, and Water.

Working volunteers receive daily Food Vouchers. These vouchers can be used at event food booths to buy meals. They are redeemable only to designated event organizations.

All volunteers agree to the Oregon Country fair Guidelines and Code of Conduct. The Code of Conduct of The Oregon Country Fair is:

"*We are an association of equals. Each and* every member of our community is entitled to respectful and equitable treatment by all other participants. We should all act responsibly towards one another wherever we gather. The OCF is committed to the principles of non-violence. Mental, verbal, physical, or sexual abuse will not be tolerated. We share reverence for the land. Stewardship is everyone's responsibility. Please help protect the plant and animal life whose space we share, and work to extend this practice beyond the OCF and into daily life."

History of the Land

The Willamette Valley has been continuously occupied by humans, to some extent, for at least the last 9,000-10,000 years (this timeline is based on the archaeological evidence gathered from 34 archaeological sites in the Upper Willamette Valley).

The Oregon Country Fair property has archaeological sites protected by state law on it. It is thought to have previously been a gathering place for the Kalapuya tribe of Native Americans. All ground disturbing activities on the fair property must be approved by the archaeology and construction crews.

The Kalapuya lived in permanent winter homes and migrated throughout the Willamette Valley of Oregon during the summers. Subsistence was based on fishing, hunting, and gathering wild plant foods.

Based on the translation of Kalapuya texts, strong historical aspects of the Kalapuya culture include: the dream, the dream spirit-power, death, wealth, prestige, sexual division of labor (men hunt, women gather), sex, acculturation, and language. The dream spirit-power was observed to be the strongest. The dream power was constantly referred to in matters of courage and bravery, of sickness and resisting disease, gambling, hunting, wealth, casting spells, power over natural phenomena and becoming a shaman.

Much of the fair site is a wetland and the Long Tom River floods much of the fair property each winter.

Educational Areas

Some of the Oregon Country Fair's areas are organized to be information and workshop resources. The *Kids Loop* is a children's play area, *Yes You Canopy* is a pavilion dedicated to the teaching of juggling, *Energy Park* is an area with displays and demonstrations on alternative energy, alternative transportation, organic agriculture and recycling, and *Community Village* has booths from non-profit organizations dedicated to education, information access, plants and gardening, including a display by the Oregon State

University/Lane County Extension Master Gardeners, and other forms of progressive social change.

Archaeology Park ("Ark Park") is the home of the fair's archaeology crew, and includes replica cedar houses like those used by Pacific Northwest Native American tribes, displays of artifacts and photos of archaeological digs from the fair site, and hands-on demonstrations of flintknapping, firemaking, basket weaving and other Native American skills.

Philanthropy

The OCF organization maintains close ties with the Eugene-area community and supports many other nonprofit organizations through its philanthropic programs.

Fairgoers, fair working volunteers, and the OCF organization alike contribute to non-profit groups through *The Jill Heiman Vision Fund*. This fund grants funds to tax-exempt organizations in Lane County. Donations are provided to projects and programs related to improving the environment and fostering sustainability.

The OCF Board has created *The Bill Wooten Endowment Fund* to assist arts, environmental, and social justice projects. The Board of Directors also offers donations to various groups and activities that share its values of living artfully and authentically on the earth.

Sideshow

In America, a sideshow is an extra, secondary production associated with a circus, carnival, fair or other such attraction.

There are four main types of classic sideshow attractions:

The "Ten-in-One" offers a program of ten sequential acts under one tent for a single admission price. The ten-in-one might be partly a freak show exhibiting "human oddities" (including "born freaks" such as midgets, giants or persons with other deformities, or "made freaks" like tattooed people, fat people or "human skeletons"- extremely thin men often "married" to the fat lady, like Isaac W. Sprague).

However, for variety's sake, the acts in a ten-in-one would also include "working acts" who would perform magic tricks or daredevil stunts. In addition, the freak show performers might also perform acts or stunts, and would often sell souvenirs like "giant's rings" or "pitch cards" with their photos and life stories.

The ten-in-one would often end in a "blowoff" or "ding," an extra act not advertised on the outside, which could be viewed for an additional fee. The blowoff act would be described provocatively, often as something deemed too strong for women and children, such as pickled punks.

The "Single-O" is a single attraction, for example a single curiosity like the "Bonnie and Clyde Death Car" or Hitler's staff car , a "Giant Rat" (actually usually a nutria) or other unusual animal, a "What Is It?" (often a convincing but artificial monstrosity like the Fiji Mermaid) or a geek show often billed as "See the Victim of Drug Abuse."

A "Museum Show" which might be deceptively billed as "World's Greatest Freaks Past and Present," is a sideshow in which the exhibits are usually not alive. It might include tanks of piranhas or cages with unusual animals, stuffed freak animals or other exotic items like the weapons or cars allegedly used by famous murderers.

Some of the exhibits might even be dummies or photographs of the billed attractions. It could still be truthfully billed with the claim "$1,000 reward if not absolutely real — please do not touch or feed the animals on exhibit". The Single-O and the Museum Show are usually operated as "grind shows," meaning that patrons may enter at any time, viewing the various exhibits at their leisure.

A "Girl Show" was sometimes offered in which women were the primary attraction. These could range from the revue (such as a "Broadway Revue") with fully-clothed performers to the racier "kootch" or "hootchie-kootchie" show (a strip show) which might play either partly clothed or "strong" (nude).

Sideshow Arts

"Working acts" often exhibited a number of stunts that could be counted on to draw crowds. These stunts used little-known methods and offered the elements of danger and excitement. Although the mainstream media often explained fanciful methods of performing these acts, the real secret was usually that there is no secret, you just do it. Such acts included fire eating, sword swallowing, knife throwing, body piercing, lying on a bed of nails, walking up a ladder of sharp swords, and more. The renewed attention to these feats has prompted a new round of oversimplified or inaccurate explanations, leading some inexperienced people to attempt them without adequate training.

Decline and Revival

Interest in sideshows declined as television made it easy (and free) to see the world's most exotic attractions. Moreover, viewing "human oddities" became distasteful as the public conscience changed, and many localities passed laws forbidding the exhibition of freaks.The performers often protested (to no avail) that they had no objection to the sideshow, especially since it provided not only a good income for them, but in many cases it provided their only possible job. The sideshow seemed destined for oblivion, until only a few exemplars of the ten-in-one remained. A greater number of "Single O" attractions still tour carnivals.

In the early 1990s former phone salesman Jim Rose developed a modern sideshow called "the Jim Rose Circus," reinventing the sideshow with two types of acts that would attract modern audiences and stay within legal bounds. The show featured acts reviving traditional sideshow stunts and carrying some of them to extremes, and "fringe" artists (often exhibiting extreme body modification) performing bizarre or masochistic acts like eating insects, lifting weights by means of hooks inserted in their body piercings, or stapling currency to their forehead. The show drew audiences at venues unknown to old-time sideshows, like rock clubs and the 1992

Lollapalooza festival. The Jim Rose Circus held its last known performance in 2005 at the Fright Dome at Circus Circus in Las Vegas, but some of its performers still tour individually. Its success sparked a growing number of performers to revive the traditional sideshow arts, taught by sideshow veterans, and many now perform in spot engagements from rock clubs and comedy clubs to corporate events. "Sideshows by the Seashore", sponsored by Coney Island USA in Brooklyn, NY has performed since 1983, and tours under the name "Coney Island Circus Sideshow".

Circus Historian and collector Ken Harck runs the Brothers Grim Sideshow, which toured with the OzzFest music festival in the summer of 2006 and 2007. In Australia, the 2007 Sydney Royal Easter Show also introduced a sideshow program amongst its attractions.

4

INTERNATIONAL HOSPITALITY FAIR IN INDIA

Athiti devo bhavah ('The guest is God' or 'Guest become God')is a Sanskrit verse, taken from an ancient Hindu scripture which became part of the "code of conduct" for Hindu society. Atithi devo bhav regards a procedure of the Host-Guest relationship. Recently it has also become the tag line of India's Ministry of Tourism's campaign to improve the treatment of tourists in India;the Indian version of Peter Drucker's customer satisfaction slogan, 'The customer is king'.

The verse is from the Taittiriya Upanishad, which says: "Matri devo bhava%, Pitri devo bhava%, Acharya devo bhava%, Athiti devo bhava%". It literally means "The Mother is God, the Father is God, the Teacher is God, [and] the guest is God."

Tithi in Sanskrit denotes a (calendrical) date. In ancient times, when means of communication were limited and it was not possible for guests to anticipate their date of arrival, "atithi" (which literally means "without a fixed calendrical time") was coined to depict a visiting person who had no fixed date of arrival or departure. "Devah" (which, through sandhi or euphonic combination, becomes written/ pronounced as "devo" when followed by certain kinds of consonants) means God and bhava% means Be or Is - "The Guest is God".

RITUAL OF POOJA

In Hinduism God is worshipped in a five step worship; this is known as *Panchopchar Poorness*. The "Shodashopchar Poojan" is an elaboration and formalisation of this ritual and involves 16 steps.

The five steps from the worship become the five formalities to be observed while receiving guests:

1. Fragrance (Dhoop) - While receiving guests the rooms must have a pleasant fragrance, because this is the first thing that attracts or detracts guests from their visit. A pleasant fragrance will put a guest in good humour.
2. Lamp (Deep) - Prior to the electrification of India, a lamp was put between host and guest so that expression and body language would remain clearly visible and therefore no gap would be created between host and guest.
3. Eatables (Naivaidya) - Fruits and sweets made of milk were offered to guests.
4. Rice (Akshat) - It is a symbol of being undivided. A *tilak,* often made of a vermilion paste, is put on the forehead and rice grains are placed on it. This is the highest form of welcome in Hindu Indian families.
5. Flower Offering (Pushp) - A flower is a gesture of good will. When the guest departs, the flower symbolizes the sweet memories of the visit that stay with them for several days.

Campaign by the Government of India

India attracts millions of tourists each year, 3.3 million in 2003, but lags far behind other destinations.To attempt to improve the number of tourists travelling to India, the Tourism Department of India started the *Atithi devo bhavah* campaign with the theme **The Incredible India.**

'Atithi Devo Bhavah' is a Social Awareness Campaign aimed at providing the inbound tourist a greater sense of being welcomed to the country. The campaign targets the general public, while focusing mainly on the stakeholders of the tourism industry. The Campains provides training and orientation to taxi drivers, guides, immigration officers, police and other personnel who interact directly with the tourist.

Bollywood actor Aamir Khan is the brand ambassador of the 'Atithi Devo Bhavah' campaign for the Ministry of Tourism.

Internationa5l Hospitality Fair

Indian hospitality is legendary as Indians always put their guests before themselves and offer the best of what they have. To create awareness and to display advancements in Indian hospitality, the Confederation of Indian Industry (CII) is organizing the International Hospitality Fair 2010 (IHF). International Hospitality Fair 2010, is a premier trade exhibition for the hospitality industry in India and serve as an ideal platform for the hospitality industry to showcase its very best in products, technology and services and new innovations to the Indian market. Following the success of the two exhibitions on Indian Hospitality, this upcoming event will be the 3rd edition of this successful series and was held from 21st to 23rd October 2010 at Pragati Maidan, New Delhi.

International Hospitality Fair 2010 was the meeting ground for more than 150 national & international exhibitors. It will provide ample opportunities for the hospitality industry to meet the sourcing needs in the areas of Food & Beverage, Housekeeping, Equipment, Interior & Fixtures, Engineering & Technology.

The targeted exhibitors at India International Hospitality Fair 2010 included the producers, manufacturers, exporters and marketers of: Hotel & Catering Equipment, Coffee Machines, Juice Machines, Chillers, Display Cabinets, Tableware, etc.

Highlights & Benefits

An exclusive International B2B Event

Over 150 Exhibitors will showcase latest products

A dazzling display of innovative products from around the world

Opportunity to meet qualified buyers seeking hospitality products/ solutions from India and Overseas

Most influential and longest established professional design event

Access a thriving market that has more ongoing development and refurbishment projects than any other region in the world

Get an opportunity to highlight and promote your company along with other top world class brands

Puskar Mela

It is the world's largest camel fair, which hosts around 50000 camels in this huge event. The camels are decorated, sold, raced and also shaved. A whole celebration of camels, a place where they enjoy their true importance- Pushkar Fair. Pushkar is a place in the Indian state of Rajasthan; the event is a big and famous thing among people everywhere in the whole world. It pulls so many people from the world that the population of the place increases to 2 lacks from a mere fourteen thousand when the fair is on.

Though small but beautiful town of Pushkar is set in a valley just about 11 km off Ajmer. It is Surrounded by hills on the three sides and sand dunes on the fourth, this place takes a very fascinating location and a just the perfect backdrop for the annual religious and cattle fair. The fairs which are famous worldwide and pull thousands of visitors from all around the globe.

A tour to Rajasthan is not complete without this. This happens once a year and it is a five-day fair. Considered very sacred and holy by the villagers around, the fair is a relaxing time for the villagers in and around the city. A very colorful fair, with men and women dressed in so many colors. Such a colorful sight is a relaxing and soothing sight for the eyes that see all arid deserts all around.

The large well touched turbans of the males visiting the place, who set their animals for trade or to set up other trade forms, such as shops selling goods, the women dressed up in well decked up ghagharas (skirts which just touch the ankle), arms full of bangles, well jeweled from head to toe in different kinds of jewellery. The typed jewellery of Rajasthan which adds a lot of charm to their dressing and intrigues the visitor.

It is an occasion which gives the Hindu pilgrims a chance to wash away their sins and wrong doings by going for a holy dip in the sacred Pushkar Lake. Pushkar happens to be one of the five dhams held with high esteem of pilgrimage spots. As per a legend, the Pushkar Lake happens to be surrounded by at least 52 palaces and 500 temples. This was for several kings and other royal in those times, who would maintain this place for pilgrimage.

Pushkar also has the only Brahma Temple of the country; this is a very important place for the Hindus and hence holds a high level of importance among the devotees.

Pushkar, provides a lot of avenues to recreate and shop, the market is huge in the times of fair, we can see people from nearby areas trading their goods, which are mostly the specialty of the particular place, such as the bead necklaces of Nagaur, woolen blankets of Marta, textiles printed in Ajmer and Jodhpur and so much more. During the fair, cultural shows and exhibitions are organized to enliven the event.

The place can be easily visited with the help of tour operators, a must visit if on tour to Rajasthan, it is indeed an experience not easy to forget.

India International Trade Fair

The India International Trade Fair, ever since its inception in 1980 has evolved as a major event for the Business community. It is a premier event organized by the India Trade Promotion Organization (ITPO), the nodal trade promotion agency of the Government of India. The event is held between 14 - 27 November every year at Pragati Maidan, New Delhi, India.

IITF is a major tourist attraction and lakhs of people visit the fair every year. This annual event provides a common platform for the manufacturers, traders, exporters and importers. The fair displays comprises a wide range of products and services including Automobiles, Coir Products, Jute, Textiles, Garments, Household Appliance, Kitchen Appliances, Processed food, Beverages, Confectionery, Drugs, Pharmaceuticals, Chemicals, Cosmetics, Bodycare & Health care products, Telecommunication, Power sector, Electronic Sector, Furniture, Home Furnishings, Sports Goods, Toys, Engineering Goods etc.

The participation figures verify the huge worldwide response of IITF. The 26th edition of IITF(2006) had around 7500 national and 350 international exhibiting companies. The fair attracted a huge audience of more than 3 million general visitors & 2,75,000 business visitors including 91 delegations from 53 countries. In fact, all business avenues will be encouraged to participate, to represent India in its totality and open fresh avenues for major business expansions.

CULTURAL EVENT IN AULI

Ski

Auli is starting to get popular among the ski-lovers. Though the long,tiring travel and unpredictable weather can be the mood killer. You cannot be sure till you reach what to expect. Few lucky can gets to enjoy snow fall and skiing. If luck is not on your side snow storm can lock your room for days. For some its hard solid snow which take away the skiing pleasure. Though the GMVNL has imported snow beater it cannot give the experience of fresh snow. There is a long Ski-Lift connecting lower slopes to the Top.

Artificial Lake

The world's highest man-made lake is at Auli, right next to the private hotel, Clifftop Club. The government has developed this in view of creating artificial snow on the new ski slopes in the event of low snow fall. The water from this lake will be used to feed the snow guns stationed along the ski slopes and thus provide a good skiing surface and exend the ski season.

Views

Auli is surrounded by high peaks like Mana, Kamet and tallest of all Nanda Devi. The 270 degree view will be enough to make you forget the long and tiring ride to reach Auli. Once the Skiing is over the best thing one can do in evening is to take chair out and get treated to great view of snow clad mountains as they keep changing colors every minute the sun goes down.

Here you will understand why the Sadhus(sage) came to Himalayas for meditation. The feeling of solitude and oneness with god will do wonders to you mind and have a positive effect on you body. You will get which no money can buy "Peace of Mind"

Trekking

Apart from skiing there are some trek options available and below list is some of the trail normally completed in single day Auli - Gorson around 7 km Gorson - Tali around 6 km Tali - Kuari Pass around 11 km Kuari Pass - Khulara around 12 km Khulara - Tapovan around 9 km

Spiritual

The place Auli is surrounded by the mighty peaks of Himalayas. Most of them have some name of goddess or some mythological connection. The one that stand out is beautiful Mt Nanda Devi which stands 7,817 Mts (25,643 ft) in height. Even the Mt Neelkant visible. Auli lies in the way of the Badrinath route. So in winter there is a heavy snow fall in Badrinath and the temple is closed for 5–6 months. During this period the deity of Lord Badri Vishal is brought and kept in temple at Joshimath. This is golden chance for Hindus and not to be missed. In Auli there is a small Hanuman temple having some connection to Ramayana.

The belief of people is when Laxman, younger brother of Lord Rama got injured fighting the Rakshas in Lanka (Sri Lanka). A medic ordered that only the herb name 'Sanjivani' found on Sanjivani mountain in Himalayas can save Laxman. Lord Rama ordered Hanuman the task. Hanuman flew from Lanka and during his way to Sanjivani mountain, he took some rest in Auli before continuing his journey.

Others

There is a training facility of Indo Tibetan Border Police. This force is responsible for guarding Indian borders at high altitude. They are subjected to hard training and its amazing to see their stamina and skiing skills. This center is equipped with best medical team for any emergency and tourist can use their help. If tourist gets trapped then the chopper service can be requested for rescue or transfer to city medical facilities.

A Hydro Power project can be seen from Auli. A private company has trapped the flowing river Alaknanda and diverted its waters through a big tunnel that runs under the mountain and the force acquired is used to generate electricity. To see this you will have to travel some 5 km towards Badrinath.

Places Around Auli

Vishu Prayag, Its an holy confluence of river Alaknanda and Dauli Ganga. It is access from the Joshimath.

Joshimath, derives from the word 'Jyotirmath' the place of Jyotirlinga of Shiva. Shankracharya founded one of the four piths "Centres' for sanyashis here. It is the resting place for the pilgrims going to Badrinath. This is a sacred place for the believers of Badrinath better known as God Vishnu. Joshimath has a temple of Narsimha, an incarnation of Vishnu.

Badrinath One of the four Dhaams. Very important for Hindus and who worships God Vishnu. Its closed in winter.

Tapovan 'Tapo' meaning meditation, 'van' means forest in Sanskrit. The place is 15 km from Joshimath and has a temple and a natural hot water spring.

Adventure Sports

Skiing is a major pastime in Auli. Facilities for skiing are available from GMVNL. There are certificate and non certificate course provided ranging from 4 days to 14 days. The courses includes stay, food, ski gear charges and guide. There are local people who provide Ski Equipment for the casual tourist and also help them to ski. If you have a weeks time, then it is possible to enroll in Ski courses and learn from experts.

Haridwar with Discovery Hospitality

Haridwar in Uttranchal of is a very holy and religious city for Hindus. At Haridwar Sacred River Ganges enters into the plains from Himalayas. Haridwar is well known for world famous kumbh mela or kumbh fair. Kumbh Mela is held at different places at different times.

The Maha Kumbh Mela is held every 12 years in one of the four pilgrim cities - Haridwar, Allahabad, Ujjian or Nasik. Millions of devotees ritually have a cleansing bath to wash their sins in the holy rivers on eleven auspicious days from the beginning of January to the end of April (we have listed auspicious dates below.

The Maha Kumbh Mela (Great Festival of Urn), takes place every after 12 years at one of the 4 religious cities (Haridwar, Allahabad, Ujjain and Nashik. This year Maha Kumbh fair is taking place at sacred town of Haridwar and is largest human gathering in history. Although very few people have heard about this in the Western Countries. Maha Kumbh Mela 2010 will have millions of pilgrims attending this religious festival between January 2010 and end April, 2010.

Keeping importance of this religious gathering in mind and the facilities available at Haridwar for visiting people. We "Discovery Hospitality" has decided to move further and set a tented camp at a convenient location at Haridwar to facilitate incoming tourist traffic to this fair.

The normal Kumbh Mela is celebrated every 3 years, the *Ardh* (half) Kumbh Mela is celebrated every six years at

Haridwar and Prayag,the *Purna* (complete) Kumbh takes place every twelve years, at four places (Prayag (Allahabad), Haridwar, Ujjain, and Nashik). The *Maha* (great) Kumbh Mela which comes after 12 'Purna Kumbh Melas', or 144 years, is held at Allahabad.

The last Ardh Kumbh Mela was held over a period of 45 days beginning in January 2007, more than 70 million Hindu pilgrims took part in the Ardh Kumbh Mela at Prayag, and on January 15, the most auspicious day of the festival of Makar Sankranti, more than 5 million participated.

The previous *Maha Kumbh Mela,* held in 2001, was attended by around 60 million people, making it at the time the largest gathering anywhere in the world in recorded history.

Kumbha Mela is a massive pilgrimage in which Hindus gather at the Ganges river. It is celebrated at different locations depending on the position of the planet of B[haspati (Jupiter) and the sun. When Jupiter and the sun are in the zodiac sign Leo (Simha Rashi) it is held in Trimbakeshwar, Nashik; when the sun is in Aries (Mesha Rashi) it is celebrated at Haradwar; when Jupiter is in Taurus (Vrishabha Rashi) and the sun is in Capricorn (Makar Rashi) Kumbha Mela is celebrated at Prayag; and Jupiter and the sun are in Scorpio (Vrishchik Rashi) the Mela is celebrated at Ujjain. Each site's celebration dates are calculated in advance according to a special combination of zodiacal positions of Sun, Moon, and Jupiter.

Kumbha is a Sanskrit word for Pitcher (actually a roundish pot with no handles), sometimes referred to as the Kalasha. It is also a zodiac sign in Indian astrology for Aquarius, the sign under which the festival is celebrated, while *Mela* means 'a gathering' or 'a meet', or simply a fair.

History

The first written evidence of the Kumbha Mela can be found in the accounts of Chinese traveler, Huan Tsang or Xuanzang (602 - 664 A.D.) who visited India in 629 -645 CE, during the reign of King Harshavardhana. However, the observance dates back many centuries to ancient India's

Vedic period, where the river festivals first started getting organised. In Hindu mythology, its origin is found in one of the popular creation myths, the *Samudra manthan* episode (Churning of the ocean of milk), mentioned in the Bhagavata Purana, Vishnu Purana, the Mahabharata, and the Ramayana.

The account goes that the Gods had lost their strength, and to regain it, they thought of churning the Ksheera Sagara (primordial ocean of milk) for amrita (the nectar of immortality). This required them to make a temporary agreement with their arch enemies, the demons or Asuras, to work together with a promise of sharing the nectar equally thereafter. However, when the *Kumbha* (urn) containing the amrita appeared, a fight ensued. For twelve days and twelve nights (equivalent to twelve human years) the gods and demons fought in the sky for the pot of amrita. It is believed that during the battle, Lord Vishnu flew away with the Kumbha of elixir spilling drops of amrita at four places: Prayag, Haridwar, Ujjain and Nashik.

Attendance

According to *The Imperial Gazetteer of India,* an outbreak of cholera occurred at the 1892 Mela at Haridwar leading to the rapid improvement of arrangements by the authorities and to the formation of Haridwar Improvement Society. In 1903 about 400,000 people are recorded as attending the fair. During the 1954 Kumbh Mela stampede at Allahabad, around 500 people were killed, and scores were injured. Ten million people gathered at Haridwar for the Kumbh on April 14, 1998.

The 1998 Kumbh Mela saw over 10 million pilgrims visiting Hardwar, to take a dip in the holy Ganges river. In 2001, around 1 million people from outside of India and from around the world participated in the *Maha Kumbh Mela* at Prayag (Allahabad), with a total participation of approximately 60 million. This mela was unusually significant due to the planetary positions at the time, a pattern that repeats only once every 144 years.

The Ritual

The major event of the festival is ritual bathing at the banks of the river in whichever town it is being held.Nasik has registered maximum visitors amounted nearly to 75 million. Other activities include religious discussions, devotional singing, mass feeding of holy men and women and the poor, and religious assemblies where doctrines are debated and standardized. Kumbh Mela is the most sacred of all the pilgrimages.

Thousands of holy men and women attend, and the auspiciousness of the festival is in part attributable to this. The sadhus are seen clad in saffron sheets with ashes and powder dabbed on their skin per the requirements of ancient traditions. Some, called *naga sanyasis,* may not wear any clothes even in severe winter.

After visiting the Kumbh Mela of 1895, Mark Twain wrote:

"It is wonderful, the power of a faith like that, that can make multitudes upon multitudes of the old and weak and the young and frail enter without hesitation or complaint upon such incredible journeys and endure the resultant miseries without repining. It is done in love, or it is done in fear; I do not know which it is. No matter what the impulse is, the act born of it is beyond imagination, marvelous to our kind of people, the cold whites."

Recent Kumbh Melas

1894

According to Paramahansa Yogananda in his work the *Autobiography of a Yogi,* it was on the Kumbha Mela in January 1894 at Prayag that his Guru Sri Yukteswar met Mahavatar Babaji for the first time.

2001

In 2001, Kumbh Mela was held in Allahabad. It is estimated that about 60 million people took a bath in the river Ganges on the occasion.

2003

When the Kumbh Mela was held in Nashik, India, from July 27 to September 7, 2003, 39 pilgrims (28 women and 11 men) were trampled to death and 57 were injured. Devotees had gathered on the banks of the Godavari river for the *maha snaan* or holy bath. Over 30,000 pilgrims were being held back by barricades in a narrow street leading to the Ramkund, a holy spot, so the sadhus could take the first ceremonial bath. Reportedly, a sadhu threw some silver coins into the crowd and the subsequent scramble led to the stampede.

2007

More than 30 million people visited Ardh Kumbh Mela at Prayag (also known as Allahabad).

2010

Haridwar hosted the Purna Kumbha mela from Makar Sankranti (14 January 2010) to *Shakh Purnima Snan* (28 April 2010). Millions of Hindu pilgrims attended the *mela*. On April 14, 2010, alone approximately 10 million people bathed in the Ganges river. According to officials by mid April about 40 million people had bathed since January 14, 2010. Hundreds of foreigners joined Indian pilgrims in the festival which is thought to be the largest religious gathering in the world. To accommodate the large number of pilgrims Indian Railways ran special trains. At least 5 people died in a stampede after clashes between holy men and devotees.

Indian Space Research Organisation took satellite pictures of the crowds with the hope of improving the conduct of the festival in the future.

Future Venues

- The Purna Kumbha Mela will again be held at Prayag in the year 2013 (January 27 to February 25)
- Nasik will host the Ardha Kumbha Mela in 2015 (August 15 to September 13)
- Ujjan Purna Kumbh Mela 2016 (April 22 to May 21)

Kumbh Mela in Media

Amrita Kumbher Sandhane, a 1982 Bengali feature film directed by Dilip Roy, documents the Kumbh Mela. Kumbha Mela has been theme for many a documentaries, including *"Kumbh Mela: The Greatest Show on Earth"* (2001) by, On 24 Sept, The Hindu reported the great faith in god displayed in kumbh mela at Nasik which had more than 70 million visitors in 2003 kumbh mela. (2004), by Maurizio Benazzo and Nick Day, *Kumbh Mela: Songs of the River* (2004), by Nadeem Uddin, and *Invocation, Kumbha Mela* (2008)

Bollywood movies often jokingly refer to Kumbh Mela as a place where the character lost his/her twin brother/sister.The most common script line being in Hindi "Hum bachpan me kumbh ke mele me kho gaye the". This is a common parody in recent times, being an effect of many movies using this lost-and-found device in the past.

On April 18, 2010, a popular American morning show The CBS Sunday Morning gave an extensive coverage on Haridwar's Kumbh Mela "The Largest Pilgrimage on Earth". Calling it "one of the most extraordinary displays of faith on Earth, a spectacular journey drawing tens of millions of people".

On April 28, 2010, BBC reported an audio and a video report on Kumbh Mela, titled "Kumbh Mela 'greatest show on earth'.

On September 30, 2010, the Kumbh Mela featured in the second episode of the Sky One TV series "An Idiot Abroad" with Karl Pilkington visiting the festival.

Faguli Festival

Introduction to Faguli

Himachal Pradesh is a North Western state in India. This state is located on the inner lap of the Western part of the Himalayan ranges. This is one of the most spectacular hill states of India. Jammu and Kashmir, Uttar Pradesh, Haryana and Punjab creates the boundary in North, South- East, South and West of Himachal Pradesh, respectively. Himachal Pradesh is packed with stunning natural beauty and this state celebrates a number of fairs and festivals in different months. Among these festivals Faguli is an important one celebrated in Himachal Pradesh. Faguli in Himachal Pradesh is related to the Basant Panchami festival. This festival takes place in the Kinnaur district. This festival celebrates the triumph of God over the evil spirit. It is the honor and tribute given by the local tribes to the God who won the battle to protect humanity.

Time of Celebrating Faguli

Faguli is a festival which is celebrated in the spring season. This religious festival of Himachal Pradesh is celebrated with another festival called Basant Panchami by the tribal people of the state. Approximately in the month of March, Faguli is celebrated in Himachal Pradesh. After the winter season almost all the people of Himachal Pradesh engage themselves in performing the rituals of Faguli in a perfect manner.

Description of Faguli Festival

Faguli Festival is the celebration of the win of the God over Evil. At the time of the festival, the local people of Himachal Pradesh engage themselves in the preparation of the festival. They clean up their homes and greet the rain Gods, chanting their name. After cleaning the home every person shoots a dart at the picture of Ravana. According to the myth if the arrow strikes the wall of the house it is considered as the mark of the God's victory over the evil spirit. In this festival the use of conch shells is prohibited.

This is because the local people believe that it may break the concentration of God during the battle with Evil Powers. On the day of Faguli the family members bring a special kind of wood called Suskar Horing at the early morning. During the evening of the Faguli festival local people burn this wood inside the caves. During the burning of wood the lard is placed on the top of the roof. At the same time the barley is baked inside the fire. According to the local belief if the baked barley grains leap up and touch the roof of the cave it is lucky for human beings. After the completion of the ceremony the local people return to the village, marching. In this procession, they follow a pattern. In front of the line there is a person with Huri, after that comes Lankawalla and then comes Kittewalla with a Doo. This Doo is seized and offered to the pet animals after completing the three rounds of the village temple. Faguli in Himachal Pradesh is also called Savani and in this festival animals are offered food for seven days.

Khogal Festival

Introduction to Khogal Festival

Himachal Pradesh the land that takes pride in its stunning landscapes, simple and religious people, presence of numerous local deities, colorful celebrations, tourist attractions has become a regular haunt among every tourist, domestic and foreigners. However of all, the thing that has truly earned immense favors and created special place in the hearts of the tourists is the celebration of various fairs and festivals in Himachal Pradesh. The fairs and festivals in Himachal Pradesh are celebrated with high intensity and enthusiasm. Local people dress up in vibrant traditional colors and follow numerous, some religious to the core and some fun oriented to the core, rituals. One such festival that has grown into massive popularity among tourists is Khogal, Himachal Pradesh. The Khogal in Himachal Pradesh has a religious connotation. It is celebrated with a belief that creating screams, loud drum and flute sounds along with torch light in hands will chase the evil spirits away.

Time of Celebrating Khogal

The festival Khogal, Himachal Pradesh is observed during Lahaul in the month of January. It usually takes place on a full moon day. Hence if you want to bask in the revelry of the festival Khogal Himachal Pradesh and want to see what exactly happens on this festival then visit this state during the month of January.

Description of Khogal Festival

To celebrate Khogal in Himachal Pradesh village people essentially the male members of the family unite at one single location. They gather at one house and take an exotic local drink namely 'Chakti'. The process of visiting house after house continues and they keep drinking the local specialty call Chakti. This activity continues till mid night. However after this, at mid night the drummers or say in their local language 'Chan' sit on the rooftop of a house. Sitting atop the roof of the house, the drummers play drums and flutes. This particular activity is the central part of the festival Khogal Himachal Pradesh. The sound of the drums and flutes mark the beginning of the Khogal celebrations. Further, with the sound of drums and flutes the village people run with lit torches in their hands towards their respective houses and scream. This particular act denotes chasing of the evil spirits away. However at the end of the day villagers gather every torch together and with rising flames of the torch they perform local dance. When dance around the bonfire is over every villager retire back to their home. They now worship the deities of their family along with the local deity called Baraja.

International Folk Festival

Introduction to the International Folk Festival

International Folk Festival is a renowned fiesta held in Himachal Pradesh and is visited by numerous tourists from across the globe. Fairs and Festivals form an integral part of Indian culture and Himachal Pradesh with its rich array of Fairs and Festivals tries its best to reserve the Indian custom. International Folk Festival is generally held in Kullu Valley during the month of October and this Fair is especially memorable for the wide range of materials available here. India with its rich cultural diversity presents itself by means of this fair before a larger audience. With the International Fair in Himachal Pradesh a new window is being opened before the people for communication.

Description of the International Folk Festival in Himachal Pradesh

The International Folk Festival offers an opportunity for cultural exchange. Indians find a way to display its wide array of talents in various fields. Since these talents find a good exposure during the International Folk Festival, it is an important event. The International Folk Festival at Himachal Pradesh has an economical significance as well. Since plentiful public from abroad comes here, they pour in their wealth whenever they find a splendid artifact. It is a well known fact that Indian abounds in such splendid artifacts. For this reason the wealth of the country gets a boost and the International Folk Festival in India thus offers an opportunity for economic balance of the country. Numerous goods like handicrafts, pottery are sold in the International Folk Festival. The handicrafts display the richness of Rajasthani culture and the pottery items upholds the Gujrati tradition. Contribution of items from all parts of the country makes this fair more charming. They add their respective hue associated with their home state and thus adds a new feather to the gorgeous coronet of the International Folk Festival in Himachal Pradesh. Moreover the cultural programs like singing and dancing offers full fledged entertainment to the people. These songs and dances belonging to various Indian states enhance the vitality of the International Folk Festival.

Time for the Celebration of the International Folk Festival

The International Folk Festival is usually held in October amidst enormous pomp and gaiety.

Fairs in Kullu Valley

Introduction to Fairs, Kullu Valley, Himachal Pradesh

Step into the Valley of God. Celebrate the fairs of Himachal Pradesh in God's own playground – Kullu Valley. Colorfully dressed men and women crowd the streets during the Fairs. Fairs in Kullu Valley, Himachal Pradesh also indicate the rich cultural Heritage of India. The Fairs reinforce our faith in the

Supreme Being and occasion fun and frolic. They are an amusing relief to the boredom of daily existence. So, Fairs in Kullu Valley, Himachal Pradesh are visited not only by the town populace but by people of other states and countries as well. Fairs in Kullu Valley have both financial and spiritual significance associated with them. Among the well known fairs of Kullu Valley, Himachal Pradesh are Kullu Dussehra and the Birshu Fair.

Description of the Fairs, Kullu Valley, Himachal Pradesh

Kullu Valley's captivating is enhanced by its colorful Fairs. River Beas flows through Kullu Valley and on the other side of the river stands the bold and beautiful mountain range of the Himalayas. A pleasant harmony is created by the scenic elegance and the cheerful cries of men and women at the Fairs. Such a harmony during Kullu Dussehra is worth a mention. Held after the Dussehra Festival with the rest of the country, the Dussehra Fairs in Kullu Valley is a careful combination of history, ethnicity and the opulence of Indian Culture. But unlike other parts of the country, effigies of Ravana and Kumbhakarna are not burnt in the Kullu Valley during the Dussehra Festival. This is perhaps the uniqueness of Dussehra at Kullu Valley and it is evident that the Dussehra Fair at the Valley would also be unique and exquisite. Amidst extensive pomp and elegance this Fair is being held at Kullu; the merry shrieks of jolly men rebounds the mountains with equal joviality. This makes the Dussehra Fair a memorable experience. The Birshu Fair is held in every village at Kullu after the worship of the Home Gods at the advent of the New Year. It ensures blessings from God and during this time people visit the local soothsayer who predicts their fortune in the forth coming year. The colors of the costumes, the joviality of the people's heart adds a new feather to the indescribable grandeur of the Valley.

Time for the Celebration of the Fairs in Kullu Valley

The time for the celebration of the Dussehra Fair is October while Birshu Fair is usually held during April or First and Second Week of May.

Gaya-Buddhist Pilgrimage Center

Gaya is another holy dot in Bihar, famous for the International Buddhist Gathering and the rallying point is the Mahabodhi tree and the adjacent temple. The occasions are Buddha Jayanti (Buddha was born on this day, he attained enlightenment on this day and also attained Nirvana on this day) and in the month of Vaisakh (April/May) and the annual session of Dalai Lama in December. Mahavir Jayanti is celebated in April with much fanfare on the Parsvanath hill and also at Vaishali while Deo Deepawali, marking the attainment of Nirvana by Mahavira is celebrated best at Pawapuri, ten days after Deepavali.

Gaya - Pitrapaksha Mela

Arond september the sleepy town of Gaya is agog with people who come here for the famous Pitrapaksha mela or the ancestor worship typified in Sraddha ritual. It is time for the Gayalis (the descendants of Magga Brahmans who were once devotees of Shiva but later converted to Vaishnavism) to be prepared for the vedic Sraddha ceremonies or the pindan - a mandatory Hind rite that is supposed to bring salvation to the departed soul. In the early Dharmasastras, Vishnu provides a list of over 50 tirthas but it proclaims that dead ancestors pray to God for a son who would offer pinda (lymph of rice) to them at Gaya.

The tradition traces its history to the time of Buddha, who is believed to have performed the first pindan here. Turning the pages of earlier history, one comes across the Puranic legend that ascribes Gaya as one of the holiest spots of the world. The Asura, named Gaya become so powerful that the gods felt threatened and thus thought of eliminating him. As a precondition to his death, the Asura demanded that be should be buried in the holiest spot of the world. This place is Gaya.

5

INTERNATIONAL HOSPITALITY FAIR IN AUSTRALIA

A celebration of Kangaroo Island food and wine, including its supert local cheeses, honey and olive oil. There's also bands and entertainment for the kids - plus a fantastic day of racing. Wine and dine your way through the Flinders Ranges and Outback, indulging in fine regional food and wine accompanied by world-class entertainment. Ride a camel to an exclusive Candlelit Dinner or watch movies under the stars and regional cooking classes. Eat your way through the region trying great Outback dishes, collect the cook book and buy the Outback condiments to make these great dishes in your own home.

The Barossa Vintage Festival is the largest and longest running wine festival in Australia. Enjoy tastings, twilight concerts, a festival ball, literary events and much more. This is a biennial event that runs for a full week, encompassing all aspects of the Barossa community. Wineries are joined by businesses, civic groups, churches and individuals to stage the various activities that make up the festival.

Want to enjoy a weekend of gourmet delights, live music and world-class wines in gorgeous Mediterranean-style surroundings? Here, South Australia's premier chefs and restaurants have joined forces with local wineries to create mouth-watering menus complemented by great wine and live entertainment throughout the region.

Head down to one of Australia's pre-eminent red wine regions for tastings, master classes, live music, gourmet food and the famous Barrel Series Auction where the finest barrels of Cabernet Sauvignon from the previous years vintage are auctioned. This event celebrates all that makes the Coonawarra wine region and includes 30 events over three days and has a myriad events for the red wine lover.

CONFEST

ConFest is an alternative bush campout festival held in the south-eastern states of Australia at New Year and Easter. The name 'ConFest' derives from combining the words conference and festival. The festival was first held in 1976 near Canberra in the Australian Capital Territory. It was initiated and organised by former Deputy Prime Minister of Australia, Jim Cairns, his personal assistant Junie Morosi and David Ditchburn as a means of bringing together the subcultures of the alternative movement.

The first gathering was held at the Cotter Dam Reserve, southwest of Canberra. The second gathering, in 1977, was on rented farmland (Mount Oak) near Bredbo, south of Canberra. It attracted 15,000 people. The farm was subsequently purchased with the festival takings as an open community.

ConFest in its early years was a melting pot of diverse worldviews. There was great passion for a better world. Conferences at ConFest attracted up to 1000 people. Workshops were held on all aspects of well-being for people and planet Earth. Some examples were gestalt therapy, massage, politics, meditation, yoga, polyamory, mud-brick construction, geodesic domes, tantra, self-sufficiency, paganism, vegetarianism and music. At the early ConFests, a number of co-operative communities held their first meetings and, at the conclusion of the festival, they went on to find and purchase land.

The Australian Down to Earth Network (ADTEN) was formed as a loose coalition. Festivals were held in every state and territory of Australia. Three state-based organisations were formed, in Victoria, Queensland, and New South Wales. They organised further festivals, usually on forested private land bordering a river. Only the Victorian Down to Earth co-operative (DTE) incorporated and has survived and it continues to organise ConFests in northern Victoria and southern New South Wales.

In 1995, the emerging trance dance movement first organised overnight outdoor doofs at ConFest following a series of amplified staged music events in the previous years. From 1995-1999 there was a period of conflict about appropriate music technologies at ConFest and amplified music was perceived by many to interrupt other activities at ConFest. ConFest music is now acoustic and campout doofs run independent of ConFests.

Landowners' concerns about public liability resulted in suitable land for sites being extremely difficult to find and DTE Victoria consequently purchased land on Gulpa Creek near Deniliquin in NSW in 2002 and held a series of ConFests on that site. DTE purchased a property on the Edwards River near Moulamein in 2006, which has since been the site for a number of Confests.

Current Scenario

Typically around 2500 people attend ConFest with new-comers and old-timers describing ConFest as alive and well.International visitors from Europe, the Middle East, SE Asia, Oceania and the Americas say there is nothing like ConFest anywhere else in the world.Recent visitors from Bougainville, Cambodia and the Philippines are exploring ways to adapt ConFest in their cultures.The majority of ConFest attendees come from Melbourne. Others come from around Australia.

Attendees at ConFest typically are interested in alternative and better futures for themselves, others and planet Earth. Workshops are run on a self-organising do-it-yourself basis. Around 12 workshops spaces are set up by site set-up volunteers and typically another 10 workshop spaces emerge. At ConFest, typically between 250 and 350 workshops and events occur.An open-stage concert is typically held on at least one evening and large drum circles play on some evenings. Fire twirling is a feature. The Art Village, energized by two ConFesters supported by others, provides a communal hot tub, steam room, massage area, life drawing and ceramics beside a ConFest beach swimming area. Around 30 massage tables are in constant use.

Confest is particularly attractive to families as it is a cheap adventure filled holiday for the kids.The summer confest tends to be more about swimming and relaxing. The Easter confest tends to be more about workshops. Anyone can put on a workshop about anything at confest - that is both the strength and weakness of the workshops!

Nights are great fun at confest with most people choosing either to hang out in the Chai Tent, drum or dance the night away or go to sleep early! Confest is requested to be a drug and alcohol free environment. These are not sold on site but rather brought by participants, People are free to go naked if they want at confest, with many people choosing to swim naked. It is definitely by no means a nudist festival though. The nudity at confest is what many first timers initially notice, but after a couple of days are tuned out of it.

Abuse of alcohol, drugs or any sexual harassment is not tolerated. However there is no official security so such issues tent to be 'negotiated.' Confest is unique in that all participants are unpaid volunteers. The only exception are the official auditors. In recent years the weather at Confest has sometimes been quite warm , prompting the organizers to consult the community about the idea of moving the event to Spring. In 2008, the forecast is for cooler weather.

Fireplace Restrictions

ConFest used to have hundreds of fires. DTE operates ConFest under permits from the Local Shire. Since 2006, because of extremely high fire danger, permits have been granted conditional on having fires only in especially set up fire circles in large cleared areas. Recently there have been around 16 of these fire circles each supported by a covered cooking area, tables, tap and enclosed gas cooking. Attendees are encouraged to form communities around these fire circles and share food. The Gypsy Kitchen has been vibrant and set an example for others. Participants are open to, and encouraged in evolving participant-initiated villages around fire circles.

Sound Restrictions

As of July 2009 - All electronically amplified sound is now banned at Confest except with equipment supplied and controlled by Down To Earth. This means that everyone must have permission from DTE to use anything that amplifies sound at a Confest. Parties wishing to use such equipment must adhere to set guidelines including recommended curfews.

DTE Victoria

DTE Victoria is an incorporated body under the Victorian Cooperatives Act. The change to the Victorian Cooperatives Act in the late 90s required that members of any Victoria Cooperative have to be Active Members engaged in activity directly related to a cooperatives core activity. As well, a quorum of members has to be present for meetings to take place. Previously DTE had over 1000 members many of whom never attended ConFest and DTE did not have their current addresses. Between 6 and 120 of these members would attend meetings depending on the waxing and waning of energy. As a direct result of the legislation change the number of members is currently around 50 members.

The Seeding of the Sydney ConFesters Group

A growing group from Sydney have since 2003 been evolving the Sydney ConFesters Group Gatherings. Between 200 and 300 attend its gatherings typically held three times a year over long weekends. DTE Victoria has provided around $8000 seed money per gathering which is repaid after the gathering. As well DTE provides its public liability insurance cover and tickets. These gatherings have always run at a surplus, which is used to buy equipment for their gathering.

The smaller size lends itself to community closeness. The Sydney Gatherings are evolving a unique feel. They differ from ConFest in a number of ways:

- All attendees are fed (vegan only from April 2006)
- A central fire (when permitted by authorities)
- Opening & closing circles ceremonies
- Smaller and more intimate

Sydney ConFest also has many of ConFest's features - a hot tub, steam room, concert, entry fee, welcoming tent, workshop boards & tents, camping facilities, showers and toilets.

Floriade (Canberra)

Floriade is a flower and entertainment festival held annually in Canberra's Commonwealth Park featuring extensive displays of flowering bulbs with integrated sculptures and other artistic features. The festival attracts tourists from around Australia and overseas in spring from mid September to mid October each year, and is considered the most important regular event for tourism in the Australian Capital Territory. It is also called "Australia's Celebration of Spring". After some controversy regarding an entry charge, admission to Floriade has been free for a number of years.

Floriade started in 1988 as a one off celebration of Canberra's 75th birthday and Australia's bicentenary of European settlement. Due to the success and popularity of the event, it has run every year since then with each year having a new theme and is currently the largest flower festival in the Southern hemisphere with over 300,000 visitors each year.

In September 2005 ACT tourism authorities considered legal action over a trademark violation with Hunter Valley

Gardens in New South Wales who had renamed their annual floral festival to *Floriade Hunter Valley Gardens*. The term Floriade was replaced with *Festival of Flowers* in 2006.

Location

Floriade is located in Commonwealth Park, Canberra.

Dates:

- 2008: 13 September - 12 October
- 2009: 12 September - 11 October

Public Art and Culture

Floriade gives great expression to public art, each year commissioning works which are placed in the Floriade gardens. Some remain beyond the festival. Floriade also showcases musical displays with many live performances, cultural celebrations, artistic displays, entertainment and recreational activities.

Floriade has also held a gnome decorating competition and display for several years, with strong participation from schools, aged people's homes, and businesses. The 2005 theme of Rock 'n Roll only accentuated the regular theme of decorating gnomes as the members of bands. Examples shown below are the Australian children's entertainers, The Wiggles, in this case renamed The Gniggles, and the crowd favorite, KISS submitted by Weetangera Primary School.

National Folk Festival (Australia)

The National Folk Festival, "The National" or "The Nash" is a five-day festival celebrating Australian folk culture, held each year on the Easter long weekend at Exhibition Park in Canberra.

The festival was conceived and first held in Melbourne in 1967.The Victorian Folk Music Club, The Monash Traditional Music Society, the Burwood Teachers Folk Club and performers Martin Wyndham Reed and Glen Tomasetti got together to orgnaise the event, inspired by the Newport Folk Festival in the United States.

From 1969 until 1991 the festival traveled to different cities each year. It was hosted at least once in Melbourne, Sydney, Adelaide, Canberra, Brisbane, Fremantle, Alice Springs, Perth, Kurunda and Maleny. The increasing size of the festival made it harder for the hosting states to organise the festival every year, so since 1992 the festival has been held in Canberra. However each year a state is 'featured' which entitles it to a proportionally larger number of entertainers, and discounted tickets for entry.

Main Features

The Festival takes place in an exhibition centre which for the duration resembles a small village of music and dance venues, cafes, and stalls. Camping is provided adjacent to the Festival grounds. In 2009, there were about 50,000 visitors. Upwards of three hundred volunteers make the festival possible. The festival has over 100 concerts, plus numerous impromptu street performances, workshops on making, playing and repairing musical instruments, storytelling and poetry, and many dance workshops. There are at least 60 craft stalls, 30+ food vendors and 2 bars. For the 5 days of the festival, there is also an almost continuous Session in the famous "Session Bar", that only stops briefly due to alcohol licence restrictions.

International and Australian performers are featured, with the organisers firmly committed to representing all kinds of Indigenous music under the banner folk music. Every night the festival has a grand dance, starting with a Scottish Ball on the Friday night, an Irish Ceili on the Saturday, and an Australian Colonial Ball on the Sunday night.

National Multicultural Festival

The National Multicultural Festival, held annually in Canberra began as a one-day event that was started by the ACT Ethnic Communities Council in 1980.

In 1997, the newly established ACT Office of Multicultural Affairs staged the first week-long Festival as a means of celebrating Canberra and Australia's cultural diversity.

The Festival is an initiative of the ACT Government and is administered by the Office of Multicultural Affairs and Community Development, a division of the Department of Disability, Housing and Community Services.

Summernats

Summernats, short for Summer Nationals, is a car festival held in Canberra, Australia. Summernats is held annually, usually at the start of the year. Summernats is the best known car festival in Australia, and an event which attracts many tourists to Canberra, bringing about $12–$15 million to the ACT economy. It has increasingly been promoted as an event for families. The Summernats attendance record was set in 2005 with 119,000 people.

Summernats features many street machines with airbrushed artwork, and restored and modified cars. It is held over a four day period, with many events, with prizes in competitions such as for burnouts, parades of cars around the track, a Miss Summernats competition, and fireworks at night.

Promoter

Summernats' promoter and organiser is Chic Henry. The naming rights sponsor of Summernats is Street Machine magazine.

Venue

Summernats is held at Exhibition Park in Canberra (EPIC), corner of Flemington Road and Federal Highway, Lyneham.

Awards

Many awards are given during the course of the festival.

Grand Champion

The most prestigious award is the "Summernats Grand Champion".

- 2007: Zoltan Bodo from Ngunnawal, Australian Capital Territory, with a 1992 Holden VP series Senator;
- 2006: Aaron Fitzpatrick from Australian Capital Territory, with a gold 1969 Datsun 510 sedan .
- 2005:
    - o Deby and Gary Myers from Narrandera NSW, in a silver 1966 Ford Mustang coupe; and
    - o Dave Ritchie from Dapto NSW, in a green 1965 Ford Falcon XP coupe.

Miss Summernats

- 2007: Jenelle Smith, 19, from Canberra
- 2006: Bree Fenton, 19, from Sydney
- 2005: Tanya Lazarou, from Sydney

Show and Shine

The Summernats holds one of Australia's most prestigious Show and Shine events. Vehicles from around the nation use the Summernats to announce their arrival on the Australian scene. There are the following categories:

- Real Street, Street, Elite and Tuff Street
- Top 60 cars, Top 20 cars and Top 10 cars
- Top Judged Elite and Top Judged Street

In addition there are some awards that are highly coveted amongst the Australian vehicle modifying community:

- Master Craftsman
- High Impact
- Artistic Impression
- People's Choice

Air Brushing

Custom Air brushing is also celebrated at the Summernats, where numerous awards are handed out.

Driving Events

There is a multitude of awards handed out to entrants in cars, which are in the following categories:

- Burnout and Burnout Masters
- Grass Motorkahana
- Go to Whoa
- Grab a Flag
- Best Cruiser
- Slalom

There is also a competition that many people[who?] say is Australia's best Dyno comp. Cars are strapped to a device that measures Horsepower at the driven wheels. During the course of the Summernats many awards in different categories are handed out in the 'Dyno-cell'. In the past outright power reads of over 1000 and 1200 hp at the wheels have been registered.

Street cruises were stopped after the 2005 Summernats, following crowd control issues. However Summernats spokesman Chic Henry was quoted as saying "The situation could be compared to so many other situations in life where people may have been having a bit too much fun, maybe having a bit too much alcohol.

Big Day Out

The Big Day Out (BDO) is an annual music festival held in several cities in Australia and New Zealand in late January. It started in Sydney in 1992, spread to Adelaide, Melbourne and Perth by 1993, with the Gold Coast and Auckland joining in 1994. As of 2003, it has featured seven or eight stages (depending on the venue) accommodating popular contemporary rock music, electronic music, mainstream international acts and local acts.

The festival began in 1992 as a Sydney-only show with Violent Femmes as the headline act, along with Nirvana and a range of other foreign and local alternative music acts playing at the Hordern Pavilion. In the months preceding the event, Nirvana's *Nevermind* was released and became an international smash hit, therefore guaranteeing the success of the festival. Kurt Cobain was ill at the time of the show. In 1993, the festival was extended to include Melbourne, Perth, and Adelaide.

Since 1994, the Big Day Out has travelled annually to Auckland, the Gold Coast, Sydney, Adelaide, Melbourne and Perth during a three-week period. The tour through the southern-hemisphere summer has become "the festival overseas acts want to be on". In 1997, organisers Ken West and Vivian Lees announced they were taking a year off, causing concern that the festival was coming to an end.

American band Pearl Jam were booked to headline the 2001 tour almost 12 months in advance, as they had just started to do festivals for the first time since problems at festivals in the early 90s. On 30 June 2000 at the Roskilde Festival in Denmark, they ended their set prematurely after the crowd surged forward, crushing and fatally injuring nine people. They pulled out of the BDO, claiming that they would never play at festivals again. They did play Leeds & Reading Festivals, UK, in 2006.

The event reached the 100-shows milestone with the second of two Sydney events in 2010. With the impending milestone nearing, Lees boasted that the BDO has been able to build relationships with acts during their careers, which has become a part of the culture of BDO. *The Australian* said this has helped secure the BDO's world status and become recognised as one of the most successful and long-running rock festivals in the world, going on to say the festival is as much a part of Australian culture as the Melbourne Cup.

In 2010, the caravan of artists and crew contained 700 people, compared to the 70 who crossed Australia in 1993. West said even the Australian bands were taking bigger crews, "Through that the festival needs more production, more riders, more hotel rooms, more everything." A solid infrastructure has been built steadily over the years to help cope with the increasing demand of the festival, with requests for video mixers, back projections and backstage internet connections obviously becoming a lot more frequent than when touring began in 1993.

Due to increasing popularity of the event, in some years a second Sydney show has been held. The first time this occurred was in 2004, in recognition of the extreme popularity of Metallica. It occurred again in 2010, when Muse headlined, and also in 2011, with Tool and Rammstein headlining.

Artist Lineups

Since its inception in 1992, Big Day Out has attracted a large range of artists, with headlining acts including Nirvana, Muse, Violent Femmes, Iggy Pop and the Stooges, The Ramones, Soundgarden, Rammstein, System of a Down, Limp Bizkit, Rage Against the Machine, The Prodigy, Marilyn Manson, Foo Fighters, Metallica, Tool, Neil Young and Red Hot Chili Peppers. The annual festival has also been a launching platform for many Australian artists, with various acts performing on the tour multiple times, such as Silverchair, Powderfinger, You Am I, The Living End, Jebediah, Grinspoon, Nick Cave and the Bad Seeds, Kisschasy and Wolfmother.

Controversy

Mosh Pit Death

During the 2001 Big Day Out festival in Sydney, Jessica Michalik was crushed in a mosh pit during a performance by the band Limp Bizkit. She was revived and rushed to Concord Hospital, but died of a heart attack five days later.

The band's frontman claimed the band had attempted to take precautions that fell on deaf ears, "We begged, we screamed, we sent letters, we tried to take precautions, because we are Limp Bizkit, we know we cause this big emotional blister of a crowd". The following day, Limp Bizkit had left Australia without telling the organisers, who only discovered the band's departure through a note left at the hotel.

Senior deputy state coroner Jacqueline Milledge issued a statement saying responsibility was on the Big Day Out's promoters Creative Entertainment Australia, saying there was overwhelming evidence that crowd density was dangerous when Limp Bizkit went on stage. Limp Bizkit was also criticised in the report, Milledge saying that Durst could have taken the situation more seriously, with his comments on stage during the attempt to rescue Michalik were "alarming and inflammatory". Michalik's parents filed separate wrongful death claims naming promoters and security personal, and in one claim, Limp Bizkit. A New South Wales court dismissed the band and all parties connected with the band from the claim, finding they were not liable.

In 2005, United National Insurance sued Limp Bizkit in an attempt to avoid paying legal fees arising from Michalik's death. The company claimed in the lawsuit, which was filed on 11 August 2005, that Limp Bizkit frontman Fred Durst incited the audience at the festival to rush the stage.

On 21 January 2007, a decision was made by the organisers to discourage Big Day Out patrons in Sydney from bringing and displaying the Australian flag. The organisers said the decision was a result of recent ethno-religious tensions in Sydney, complaints that the previous year's festival had been marred by roving packs of aggressive flag-draped youths, and recognition that some indigenous Australians take issue with celebrating the start of British settlement.

Sections of the community had strong views supporting or objecting to the policy. Former Prime Minister John Howard, New South Wales Premier Morris Iemma and Federal Leader of the Opposition Kevin Rudd publicly condemned the move. Iemma suggested the event be cancelled if the organisers could not secure the safety of attendees. Main stage act Jet performed in front of a large backdrop of a black-and-white Australian flag cut-out of their name, with lead vocalist Nic Cester adding, "I can't tell anyone else what to do but we as a band are very proud to be Australian and we don't want to feel we are not allowed to feel proud".

However, other people including Andrew Bartlett of the Australian Democrats, sports writer Peter FitzSimons and members of the hip hop outfit The Herd expressed concern that the flag was being misused by a handful of aggressive attendees in a jingoist manner, and that rock concerts were not the appropriate venue to be waving a flag.

Drug Usage and Death

Drug usage is commonly associated with the Big Day Out, with police searching suspected users and dealers by placing drug sniffing dogs at some entrances of each venue and patrolling the event. At the 2008 festival in Sydney, police made 86 drug-related arrests. In 2009, identification of 258 suspects resulted in 107 people being detained for drug violations. In Perth (2009), police made 59 arrests for possession of drugs, including four with intent to sell or supply. 129 tablets of MDMA, two grams of methamphetamine, six grams of cannabis, 75 cannabis joints, and 21 tablets of dextroamphetamine were seized by police.

At the 2009 Big Day Out festival in Perth, 17-year-old Gemma Thoms collapsed after allegedly taking three ecstasy tablets. She died 12 hours later in Sir Charles Gairdner Hospital, after being transferred from the event's first-aid post. The girl and her friend reportedly took one tablet each whilst at home before the event. After arriving, she reportedly saw police near the entrance, panicked, and swallowed another two tablets. Police later denied responsibility for Thoms' death, noting that no sniffer dogs were being used to search patrons at the entrance she had used. Thoms had been driven by car and had not taken the train to the station where police were searching. Police did not make any arrests, but officers did raid a house in their search for the dealer who had supplied the ecstasy.

In addition, bands themselves have been caught in drug situations leading to death, especially in the case of Shihad, whose manager, Gerald Dwyer, died of a drug overdose in 1996 in his hotel room, just hours after watching the band's set at the Auckland BDO. The band skipped the Brisbane BDO in order to attend Gerald's funeral, and later rejoined the BDO tour in Sydney.

Beenie Man Controversy

In November 2009, gay rights groups in New Zealand protested after controversial rapper Beenie Man was included in the second round of announcements for the 2010 tour. Groups such as GayNZ.com cited controversial and homophobic lyrics from Beenie Man's songs such as "I'm dreaming of a new Jamaica/Come to execute all the gays". The group called for Big Day Out organisers to drop Beenie Man from the line up "to send a message that homophobia is unacceptable", and over 850 people joined a Facebook group to oppose his appearance.

On 15 November 2009, the festival's Australian organisers issued a statement on their website, confirming that Beenie Man had indeed been dropped from the lineup. Whilst they acknowledged his commitment to the 2007 Reggae Compassionate Act and his promises to not perform the offending songs on his tour, they ultimately made the decision to drop Beenie Man because they felt his appearance would "be divisive amongst our audience members and would mar the enjoyment of the event for many."

INTERNATIONAL HOSPITALITY FAIR IN REST WORLD

Small fairs facilitate positive interaction among tourism players, including local travel providers, community leaders, media, government officials and inspired travelers. Even better — such events are quite effective without being expensive! The difference between a traditional tourism conference or tradeshow and a grassroots events is the focus. Create something that serves the needs of locals while being receptive to visitors. Unlike a tradeshow, you are not busy scheduling talks and expos but rather you allow participants to greater control, using the materials on hand.

Since 2001, Planeta.com has partnered with friends in Oaxaca, Mexico in hosting an anual tourism event. The average cost is about $200 U.S. dollars per event. Purposefully, the budget is kept quite low so that the event can replicated elsewhere. All that's needed is plenty of good will and patience. On a sidenote, I am happy to consult with communities, local governments and business associations. The important point is that grassroots events create the opportunity to bring together multiple stakeholders. Here are some lessons learned.

BEFORE THE EVENT

Convene friendly and short meetings with partners to organize the schedule of events. Collect feedback from those interested in the fair but unlikely to attend. Can they participate in parallel events online, using Flickr, Facebook, Twitter and YouTube? Update the schedule online, preferably on a wiki. (Example: 2011 Responsible Tourism Fair) Prepare promotion — online and natural world — including a website, Flickr, Facebook, Twitter, requesting links on other websites, posting news on relevant forums and print ads (volantes) to distribute locally. Prepare materials for participants, including flyers, program, identification tags and diplomas if desired. Prepare a survey or surveys for participants.

TE MATATINI NATIONAL KAPA HAKA FESTIVAL

Kapa Haka is a combination of Maori dance and action songs performed by large groups with absolute precision. In competitions, each group is judged on specific criteria and the rivalry is fierce. This national festival has been described as the 'Olympics of Kapa Haka'. Expect to feel the hair stand on the back of your neck as you are bathed in a sea of powerful emotions.

NEW ZEALAND FRINGE FESTIVAL

Now in its 21st year, this 'art-on-the-edge' festival delivers comedy, dance, theatre, music, visual arts and more. Convention is often thrown to the wind as artists unleash their remarkable talents. Culminating in a series of awards, the New Zealand Fringe Festival has helped bring international recognition to leading Kiwi artists, such as Bret McKenzie and Jermaine Clement from Flight of the Conchords.

MERCURY BAY ART ESCAPE

Held over two long weekends, this self-drive tour of more than 35 art studios and galleries is set in the beautiful Mercury Bay area. For generations, an eclectic mix of talented painters, sculptors, jewellers, printmakers and ceramicists have made this area their home, finding inspiration in The Coromandel's lush forests, pristine white-sand beaches and close-to-nature lifestyle. Mercury Bay Art Escape is a unique opportunity to meet with the artists at their studios. You'll also be able to purchase art directly from the source. Local cafes and a boutique vineyard add to the festival with fresh food, delicious wines and live music.

ROTORUA FESTIVAL OF ARTS

The geothermal city of Rotorua erupts with a fascinating selection of visual, musical and performing arts. From the Royal New Zealand Ballet and the New Zealand Symphony Orchestra to modern dance productions, theatre and hilarious comedy, the Rotorua Festival of Arts has something for everyone. Part of the festival's vision is to create an event that is 'not too serious and pushes boundaries', so you can expect a programme filled with unique and highly entertaining experiences.

PASIFIKA FESTIVAL

This is one of the most significant events in the Pacific region. It's a huge celebration of cultural diversity with performers from Samoa, Tonga, Cook Islands, Fiji, Niue, Tahiti, Tokelau, Tuvalu, Kiribati and, of course, New Zealand Maori. The opening ceremony takes place 6 March and a programme of events around the city leads up to the main Pasifika day on 12 March. Set in a large lakeside park, you're free to wander from 'village to village' as though travelling from one Pacific nation to another. You'll discover cultural workshops, traditional food outlets, hundreds of stalls and 12 stages presenting non-stop live entertainment.

AUCKLAND ARTS FESTIVAL

Every two years the Auckland Arts Festival presents an exceptional programme of entertainment from leading international and New Zealand artists. Highlights this year include Vietnamese water puppets, Rajasthani music from India, Bolivian theatre, Taiwanese drumming, French contemporary dance, British and Mexican visual artists, and global music stars, such as Paul Kelly and Martha Wainwright. A special 'White Night' event will see galleries and museums stay open late into the night.

WOMAD NEW ZEALAND 2011

WOMAD is a three-day celebration of life in a global village. Set in a 55-acre park with natural amphitheatres, it's a truly magical picnic-style outdoor event. Numbers are limited to 12,500 each day to ensure there's plenty of space for everyone. This year, more than 300 performers from 20 countries, including New Zealand, will present 30 hours of live music on seven stages. WOMAD New Zealand 2011 will also feature attractions such as 'artists in conversation', live cooking demonstrations and artist workshops, a global village with more than 80 stalls, a sustainable village and Kidzone, a creative area for under-12s.

ID DUNEDIN FASHION WEEK

A long-established fashion subculture within Dunedin has fostered a unique look and feel. iD Dunedin Fashion Week is a celebration of the city's fashion identity, as well as a presentation of the latest collections from emerging designers and established labels. The main fashion shows at the end of the week showcase designers from around 20 labels; the catwalk is the platform of the city's historic railway station. During the week you could also catch presentations of historical collections and vintage fashion publications and listen to guest speakers from the creative sector.

ARROWTOWN AUTUMN FESTIVAL

Located at the centre of the South Island lakes district, Arrowtown is known for its historic main street and autumn displays of red, yellow and gold. The festival begins with a colourful street parade with vintage cars, dancing girls and brass bands. Daily events organised by the local community include a musical, comedy acts, jazz and country music, as well as an art and craft market, art exhibition and art-2-wear competition. At lunchtimes, performers provide free entertainment along the main street.

HORECAVA

The Horecava is a Dutch annual hospitality trade fair held in Amsterdam since 1957It is the largest hospitaly fair in the Netherlands. It hosts the annual Dutch national championship hospitality since 2007.

The initiative for a national hospitality exhibition was taken in 1953 by Gerrit Staalman, who pled for a such an exhibition in hospitaly magazine Misset Horeca, for which he was an advisor. In 1957 a first exihibition is held, organised by the Dutch Trade fair organisation. From 1959 the exposition is held in the Rai building.

The fair has since then grown to the point where only those who are professionally active in hospitality are allowed as visitors in 1995. From this year on, large brewers, coffee producers, and large kitchen exposers decide to attend the fair only bi-annually, on even years, on what is known as a "wet" Horecava, odd years being called "dry". Since 2008 Horecava tries to slowly abolish the distinction.

EXHIBITIONS

The Horecava has several exhibition areas, each with exposants from different areas in hospitality and catering. The areas are interior design, outdoors, luxury food, coffee and corporate uniforms, fresh produce, drink and music, nightlife, innovation and trends, wine professional, fast service, interior decorating, automation, hotel, and large kitchen.

Innovation

The innovation pavilion focusses on innovative products for hospitality. Since 2001 it presents an annual innovation award. The award is presented in the categories Food & Beverage, Interior & Design, and Equipment.

Wine Professional

The Wine Professional is a wine exposistion that has been held in conjunction with the Horecava since 2003. It is organised by The Wine and Food association, and is not part of the Horecava organisation.

Saint Patrick's Day

Saint Patrick's Day is a religious holiday celebrated internationally on 17 March. It is commemorates Saint Patrick (c. AD 387–461), the most commonly recognised of the patron saints of Ireland, and the arrival of Christianity in Ireland. It is observed by the Catholic Church, the Anglican Communion (especially the Church of Ireland), the Eastern Orthodox Church and Lutheran Church. Saint Patrick's Day was made an official feast day in the early 17th century, and has gradually become a celebration of Irish culture in general.

The day is generally characterised by the attendance of church services, wearing of green attire (especially shamrocks), and the lifting of Lenten restrictions on eating and drinking alcohol, which is often proscribed during the rest of the season.

Saint Patrick's Day is a public holiday in the Republic of Ireland, Northern Ireland, Newfoundland and Labrador and in Montserrat. It is also widely celebrated by the Irish diaspora, especially in places such as the Great Britain, Canada, the United States, Argentina, Australia, and New Zealand, among others.

Little is known of Patrick's early life, though it is known that he was born in Roman Britain in the 4th century, into a wealthy Romano-British family. His father and grandfather were deacons in the Church. At the age of sixteen, he was kidnapped by Irish raiders and taken captive to Ireland as a slave.

It is believed he was held somewhere on the west coast of Ireland, possibly Mayo, but the exact location is unknown. According to his Confession, he was told by God in a dream to flee from captivity to the coast, where he would board a ship and return to Britain. Upon returning, he quickly joined the Church in Auxerre in Gaul and studied to be a priest.

In 432, he again said that he was called back to Ireland, though as a bishop, to Christianise the Irish from their native polytheism. Irish folklore tells that one of his teaching methods included using the shamrock to explain the Christian doctrine of the Trinity to the Irish people. After nearly thirty years of evangelism, he died on 17 March 461, and according to tradition, was buried at Downpatrick. Although there were other more successful missions to Ireland from Rome, Patrick endured as the principal champion of Irish Christianity and is held in esteem in the Irish Church.

WEARING OF THE GREEN

Originally, the colour associated with Saint Patrick was blue. Over the years the colour green and its association with Saint Patrick's day grew. Green ribbons and shamrocks were worn in celebration of St Patrick's Day as early as the 17th century. He is said to have used the shamrock, a three-leaved plant, to explain the Holy Trinity to the pagan Irish, and the wearing and display of shamrocks and shamrock-inspired designs have become a ubiquitous feature of the day. In the 1798 rebellion, in hopes of making a political statement, Irish soldiers wore full green uniforms on 17 March in hopes of catching public attention. The phrase "the wearing of the green", meaning to wear a shamrock on one's clothing, derives from a song of the same name.

In Ireland

Saint Patrick's feast day, as a kind of national day, was already being celebrated by the Irish in Europe in the ninth and tenth centuries. In later times he became more and more widely known as the patron of Ireland. Saint Patrick's feast day was finally placed on the universal liturgical calendar in the Catholic Church due to the influence of Waterford-born Franciscan scholar Luke Wadding in the early 1600s. Saint Patrick's Day thus became a holy day of obligation for Roman Catholics in Ireland.

The church calendar avoids the observance of saints' feasts during certain solemnities, moving the saint's day to a time outside those periods. Saint Patrick's Day is occasionally affected by this requirement, when 17 March falls during Holy Week. This happened in 1940, when Saint Patrick's Day was observed on 3 April in order to avoid it coinciding with Palm Sunday, and again in 2008, where it was officially observed on 14 March (15 March being used for St. Joseph, which had to be moved from March 19), although the secular celebration still took place on 17 March. Saint Patrick's Day will not fall within Holy Week again until 2160. (In other countries, St. Patrick's feast day is also March 17, but liturgical celebration is omitted when impeded by Sunday or by Holy Week.)

In 1903, Saint Patrick's Day became an official public holiday in Ireland. This was thanks to the Bank Holiday (Ireland) Act 1903, an act of the United Kingdom Parliament introduced by Irish MP James O'Mara. O'Mara later introduced the law that required that pubs and bars be closed on 17 March after drinking got out of hand, a provision that was repealed in the 1970s. The first Saint Patrick's Day parade held in the Irish Free State was held in Dublin in 1931 and was reviewed by the then Minister of Defence Desmond Fitzgerald. Although secular celebrations now exist, the holiday remains a religious observance in Ireland, for both the Roman Catholic Church and the Church of Ireland.

In the mid-1990s the Irish government began a campaign to use Saint Patrick's Day to showcase Ireland and its culture. The government set up a group called St. Patrick's Festival, with the aim to:

— Offer a national festival that ranks amongst all of the greatest celebrations in the world and promote excitement throughout Ireland via innovation, creativity, grassroots involvement, and marketing activity.

— Provide the opportunity and motivation for people of Irish descent, (and those who sometimes wish they were Irish) to attend and join in the imaginative and expressive celebrations.

— Project, internationally, an accurate image of Ireland as a creative, professional and sophisticated country with wide appeal, as we approach the new millennium.

The first Saint Patrick's Festival was held on 17 March 1996. In 1997, it became a three-day event, and by 2000 it was a four-day event. By 2006, the festival was five days long; more than 675,000 people attended the 2009 parade. Overall 2009's five day festival saw close to 1 million visitors, who took part in festivities that included concerts, outdoor theatre performances, and fireworks.

The topic of the 2004 St. Patrick's Symposium was "Talking Irish," during which the nature of Irish identity, economic success, and the future were discussed. Since 1996, there has been a greater emphasis on celebrating and projecting a fluid and inclusive notion of "Irishness" rather than an identity based around traditional religious or ethnic allegiance. The week around Saint Patrick's Day usually involves Irish language speakers using more Irish during *seachtain na Gaeilge* ("Irish Week").

As well as Dublin, many other cities, towns, and villages in Ireland hold their own parades and festivals, including Cork, Belfast, Derry, Galway, Kilkenny, Limerick, and Waterford.

The biggest celebrations outside Dublin are in Downpatrick, County Down, where Saint Patrick is rumoured to be buried. In 2004, according to Down District Council, the week-long St. Patrick's Festival had more than 2,000 participants and 82 floats, bands, and performers and was watched by more than 30,000 people. The shortest St Patrick's Day parade in the world takes place in Dripsey, Cork. Th parade lasts just 100 yards and travels between the village's two pubs.

Christian leaders in Ireland have expressed concern about the secularisation of St Patrick's Day. In The Word magazine's March 2007 issue, Fr. Vincent Twomey wrote, "It is time to reclaim St Patrick's Day as a church festival." He questioned the need for "mindless alcohol-fuelled revelry" and concluded that "it is time to bring the piety and the fun together."

In Argentina

In Argentina, and especially in Buenos Aires, all-night long parties are celebrated in designated streets, since the weather is comfortably warm in March. People dance and drink only beer throughout the night, until seven or eight in the morning, and although the tradition of mocking those who do not wear green does not exist, many people wear something green. In Buenos Aires, the party is held in the downtown street of Reconquista, where there are several Irish pubs; in 2006, there were 50,000 people in this street and the pubs nearby. Neither the Catholic Church nor the Irish community, the fifth largest in the world outside Ireland, take part in the organisation of the parties.

In Canada

One of the longest-running Saint Patrick's Day parades in North America occurs each year in Montreal, the flag of which has a shamrock in one of its corners. The parades have been held in continuity since 1824.

In Quebec City, there was a parade from 1837 to 1926. The Quebec St-Patrick Parade returned in 2010, after an absence of more than 84 years. For the occasion, a portion of the NYPD Pipes and Drums were present as special guests.

The Toronto Maple Leafs hockey team was known as the Toronto St. Patricks from 1919 to 1927, and wore green jerseys. In 1999, when the Maple Leafs played on *Hockey Night in Canada* (national broadcast of the NHL) on Saint Patrick's Day, they wore the green St. Patrick's day-themed retro uniforms. There is a large parade in the city's downtown core that attracts over 100,000 spectators.

Some groups, notably Guinness, have lobbied to make Saint Patrick's Day a national holiday in Canada. Currently, the Canadian province of Newfoundland and Labrador is the only jurisdiction in Canada where Saint Patrick's Day is a provincial holiday.

In March 2009, the Calgary Tower had changed its top exterior lights to new green-coloured CFL bulbs just in time for Saint Patrick's Day. The lights were in fact part of the environmental non-profit organisation, Project Porchlight, and were Green to represent environmental concerns. Approximately 210 lights were changed in time for Saint Patrick's Day and almost resemble a Leprechaun's hat during the evening light. After a week, regular white CFLs took their place, saving the Calgary Tower around $12,000 and reducing greenhouse gas emissions by 104 metric tonnes in the process.

In Great Britain

In Great Britain, the Queen Mother used to present bowls of shamrock flown over from Ireland to members of the Irish Guards, a regiment in the British Army consisting primarily of soldiers from both Northern Ireland and the Republic of Ireland. The Irish Guards still wear shamrock on this day, flown in from Ireland.

Christian denominations in Great Britain observing his feast day include The Church of England and the Roman Catholic Church.

Horse racing at the Cheltenham Festival attracts large numbers of Irish people, both residents of Britain and many who travel from Ireland, and usually coincides with Saint Patrick's Day.

Birmingham holds the largest Saint Patrick's Day parade in Britain with a massive city centre parade over a two mile (3 km) route through the city centre. The organisers describe it as the third biggest parade in the world after Dublin and New York.

London, since 2002, has had an annual Saint Patrick's Day parade which takes place on weekends around the 17th, usually in Trafalgar Square. In 2008 the water in the Trafalgar Square fountains was dyed green.

Liverpool has the highest proportion of residents of Irish ancestry of any English city.This has led to a long-standing celebration on St Patrick's Day in terms of music, cultural events and the parade.

Manchester hosts a two-week Irish festival in the weeks prior to St Patrick's Day. The festival includes an Irish Market based at the city's town hall which flies the Irish tricolour opposite the Union Flag, a large parade as well as a large number of cultural and learning events throughout the two-week period. The Scottish town of Coatbridge, where the majority of the town's population are of Irish descent,also has a St. Patrick's Day Festival which includes celebrations and parades in the town centre. Glasgow began an annual Saint Patrick's Day parade and festival in 2007.

In Montserrat

The tiny island of Montserrat, known as "Emerald Island of the Caribbean" because of its founding by Irish refugees from Saint Kitts and Nevis, is the only place in the world apart from Ireland and the Canadian province of Newfoundland and Labrador where St Patrick's Day is a public holiday. The holiday commemorates a failed slave uprising that occurred on 17 March 1768.

In South Korea

Seoul (Capital city of South Korea) has celebrated Saint Patrick's Day since 2001 with Irish Association of Korea. The place of parade and festival has been moved from Itaewon and Daehangno to Cheonggyecheon.

In New Zealand

Saint Patrick's Day is widely celebrated in New Zealand - green items of clothing are traditionally worn and the streets are often filled with revellers drinking and making merry from early afternoon until late at night.

The Irish made a large impact in New Zealand's social, political and education systems, owing to the large numbers that emigrated there during the 19th century and Saint Patrick's Day is seen as a day to celebrate individual links to Ireland and Irish heritage.

In Japan

Saint Patrick's Parades are now held in 9 locations across Japan.The first parade, in Tokyo, was organised by The Irish Network Japan (INJ) in 1992. Nowadays Parades and other events related to Saint Patrick's Day spread across almost the entire month of March.

EARLY CELEBRATIONS

The Charitable Irish Society of Boston organised the first observance of St. Patrick's Day in the Thirteen Colonies. Surprisingly, the celebration was not Catholic in nature, Irish immigration to the colonies having been dominated by Protestants.[8] The society's purpose in gathering was simply to honour its homeland, and although they continued to meet annually to coordinate charitable works for the Irish community in Boston, they did not meet on the 17th of March again until 1794.[8] During the observance of the day, individuals attended a service of worship and a special dinner.[8]

New York's first Saint Patrick's Day observance was similar in nature to that of Boston's. It was held on 17 March 1762 in the home of John Marshall, an Irish Protestant, and over the next few years informal gatherings by Irish immigrants were the norm. The first recorded parade in New York was by Irish soldiers in the British Army in 1766.[9] In 1780, General George Washington, who commanded soldiers of Irish descent in the Continental Army, allowed his troops a holiday on 17 March "as an act of solidarity with the Irish in their fight for independence." This event became known as The St. Patrick's Day Encampment of 1780. Irish patriotism in New

York City continued to soar and the parade in New York City continued to grow. Irish aid societies were created like Friendly Sons of St. Patrick and the Hibernian Society and they marched in the parades too. Finally when many of these aid societies joined forces in 1848 the parade became not only the largest parade in the United States but one of the largest in the world.

CUSTOMS TODAY

In every year since 1991, March has been proclaimed Irish-American Heritage Month by the US Congress or President due to the date of St. Patrick's Day. Christian denominations in the United States observing his feast day include the Evangelical Lutheran Church in America, Protestant Episcopal Church, and the Roman Catholic Church. Today, Saint Patrick's Day is widely celebrated in America by Irish and non-Irish alike. For most Irish-Americans, this holiday is both religious and festive. St. Patrick's Day church services are followed by parades and parties, Irish music, songs, and dances. It is one of the leading days for consumption of alcohol in the United States, as individuals are allowed to break their Lenten sacrifices for the day in order to celebrate Saint Patrick's Day. Many people choose to wear green coloured clothing and items. Traditionally, those who are caught not wearing green are pinched affectionately.

Seattle and other cities paint the traffic stripe of their parade routes green. Chicago dyes its river green and has done so since 1962 when sewer workers used green dye to check for sewer discharges and had the idea to turn the river green for Saint Patrick's Day. Originally 100 pounds of vegetable dye was used to turn the river green for a whole week but now only forty pounds of dye is used and the colour only lasts for several hours.

Indianapolis also dyes its main canal green. Savannah dyes its downtown city fountains green. Missouri University of Science and Technology - St Pat's Board Alumni paint 12 city blocks kelly green with mops before the annual parade.In Jamestown, New York, the Chadakoin River (a small tributary that connects Conewango Creek with its source at Chautauqua Lake) is dyed green each year.

Columbia, SC dyes its fountain green in the area known as Five Points (a popular collegiate location near the University of South Carolina). A two day celebration is held over St Patrick's Day weekend. In Boston, Evacuation Day is celebrated as a public holiday for Suffolk County. While officially commemorating the British departure from Boston, it was made an official holiday after Saint Patrick's Day parades had been occurring in Boston for several decades, and is often believed to have been popularised because of its falling on the same day as Saint Patrick's Day.

7

GLOBAL HOSPITALITY EVENTS

Global events provides upscale corporate hospitality packages for Fortune 500 companies to over 50 events such as the Super Bowl, Final Four, 2012 Summer Games in London, and The Masters. We understand the importance of building client relationships through corporate hospitality packages and take personal care in looking after you and your guests. Global Events is the premiere company specializing in upscale corporate hospitality packages with tickets to the world's greatest events. Global Events places you, the client, first. We understand the importance of building client relationships through corporate hospitality and take personal care in looking after you and your guests with five-star treatment.

HOSPITALITY

Hospitality is about serving the guests to provide them with **"feel-good-effect" "Athithi devo bhavha"** (Guest is God) has been one of central tenets of Indian culture since times immemorial. In India, the guest is treated with utmost warmth and respect and is provided the best services, 24x7 Global Hospitality is following the same path.

Today hospitality sector is one of the fastest growing sectors in India. It is expected to grow at the rate of 8% between 2007 and 2016. Nowadays the travel and tourism industry is also included in hospitality sector. The boom in travel and tourism has led to the further development of hospitality industry.

Tour and Travel

Corporate travel management services are gaining more acceptances in corporate sector due to a variety of reasons like relocation, employee satisfaction programs etc. Global Hospitality specializes in providing latest and most popular corporate travel management services to a number of corporations, professionals, executives and frequent fliers.

You might be having business travel plans for that all important client meeting. How should you be proceeding for it? It could quite be a complex thing to negotiate air fares; book hotel accommodation and cross check your all expenditures. As it is not your core business, you cannot afford to divert your valuable human resources to do all this for you. Keeping a full time travel manager and a dedicated team for this purpose may not be a viable option as you may not be requiring such resources at all as your corporate air travel might be for a limited period of time and that too for a particular occasion or season only.

Trust Experts for Your Business Travel Solutions

It therefore makes sense that you outsource all these functions to a professional global corporate services provider who will do all the necessary home-wok for you for your business travel solutions. 24x7 Global Hospitality has a dedicated team of professionals who have years of expertise in providing customized corporate travel management services and hot travel deals to business travelers and professionals. The business travel solutions that we provide to our clients include:

- Customized business travel solutions that comply with your organizations travel policy
- Discounted Air Fares and corporate car services

- Customized Solutions for Your Complex Itineraries
- Booking of Hotel Accommodation.
- Transparency in Services Offered

Global Equipments (Hospitality Products)

Global Equipments is a leading company manufacturing kitchen equipments for service industry, and hospitals etc. It is actively responding to the needs of its clients all over the world which has helped realize its goal. As sure its clients good quality equipments, to best prices by creating better and faster production infrastructure, Global products are value for money quality products. Supplied all over the world. It is managed by a generation & professionals , teamed together for one aim of providing the best possible products & services to our client's.

The company manufactures a complete range of Kitchen Equipments from Food Preparation, Food Service, Food storage & Ware Washing with its extensive technical capability, management, innovative work force & Quality consciousness. Global has earned an exemplary capability of being the most trusted name in this industry & enjoy excellent good will through out since long. It has been made possible by sustained R & D and product improvement integrating customer feed back to shop floor level & introducing new result oriented products to the market with help of its unique widespread sales & service network, The company has professionally worked towards continuous improvement in products, procedures and services. We reserve the right to change or modify the design & specification in tune with new technology development for better performances.

SERVICES

The Organization

Global Equipments (Hospitality Products)- has been providing logistic support under strict quality control at affordable cost. The day-to-day operation is being managed by:

- Marketing & Facility Planning Department
- Production Department
- Procurement & Quality Control Department
- Logistic & After Sales Department.

All the departments are being headed by veterans experienced & competent in their respective fields & all the operations are being headed chaired & guided by our C.E.O.

Production

The entire production is separated in three phase:

1. **Procurement Section** - From procuring the raw material to stacking all needed accessories & gadgetries & placing then in proper storeroom & storing yard.
2. **Sheet Metal Section** - From getting the sheet metal from Yard to this section for cutting, bending & punching.
3. **Electrical / LPG Fitting** - After completion all the sheet metal works, the source of energy is being fitted /connected by qualified &b competent technicians.
4. **Trial Run** - After finishing each product a trial run is being carried twice to as certain the optimum results & passed on to quality controller.
5. **Inspection by Quality Controller** - After trial runs the quality controller goes through all the aspects of the equipments from sheet metal to final run to get the maximum output of the equipments.
6. **Installation & Service Manual** - After delivering of the equipment a live demonstration is being carried out to the user / working hard & instruction manual is given. The working hand is being briefed about dos & don'ts & instruction is being given to prevent any mishaps.
7. **After Sales Service** - Within the warranty period of 12 months, the organization carries out quarterly

check up of the each & all equipments & keep enquiring through after sales department about the recent state. In case of any call, the follow up is being carried out with in shortest possible time.

8. **After the Warranty Period** - After the expiry of warranty period if any call is made to us we do attend with minimum service charges & if any replacement or if any servicing is needed we do charge for the spares extra as optimum rates.

Specialized Services

We offer services in the following areas:

Kitchen Location/Sizing

- Recommending the most suitable location for kitchen with regard to raw material inlet, food service outlets, natural lighting, availability of fresh air etc.

Kitchen Planning

- Identifying the type of equipment required in the kitchen to match the menu and covers.
- Sizing and designing of food service equipment with detailed shop drawing.
- Preparing detailed specifications for all the equipment.
- Preparation of a kitchen layout to ensure proper flow of men and preparation & cooking of food etc.
- Service, dish washing, pan washing, pantry, bakery, trolley parking etc.

L.P. Gas System Designing

- Estimating the total gas requirements to run smoothly the kitchen at peak load.
- Locating the cylinder storage room and working out sizing and specifications for the same to ensure safe storage and to comply with standards.
- Sizing of L.P. Gas piping, valves, regulators and fitting.

Engineering Design for Kitchen Exhaust System

- Design data for exhaust hoods along with drawing.
- Sizing of exhaust ducting based on correct duct velocities.
- Estimating the static and dynamic head for the exhaust fan.

Our Strengths

- **Robust Infrastructure:** Global Equipments (Hospitality Products) boasts of sound infrastructure and highly skilled & dedicated workforce that enables it to cater to customer's requirement. The R&D department is equipped with the latest computer aided design (CAD) section and material testing lab. Production involves stringent quality checks resulting in flawless products.
- **Active R & D Division**: Being a progressive organization run by a team of highly experienced and well trained technocrats, the company looks forward to innovative ideas. It is constantly designing and fabricating new products as per requirements of the customers.
- **Better After Sales Services**: The company realizes the importance of effective after sales service and ensuring that customers are completely satisfied with the performance of the company's products. Therefore, round-the-clock after sales services are provided to customers through dedicated customer care development.

Global Catering Services

The group's catering division is one of the leading catering companies in the capital and the National capital region. Managed by hospitality professionals, the Global Hospitality catering division is renowned for its immaculate service and style offering the highest level of guest satisfaction and value to its esteemed clients. Once you have decided to host your function with us, all you have to do is sit back and relax. Regardless of the fact that the host invites 100 or 5000 guests, the Global Hospitality' Catering Services is committed to provide efficient and professional services to meet the guests' every need. From exquisite themes for any occasion to the best of world cuisine and service style, the catering division has the expertise to make any function a grand success.

The group has catered to many prestigious international organizations and has undertaken turn-key catering projects and consultancy services for large Industrial Houses, Public Sector Undertakings, Diplomatic Missions, Multinational companies, corporate events and International conferences.

In addition, for turn-key arrangements, the Group has its very own professional team of consultants ensuring complete peace of mind for services related to theme décor, flower arrangements, state-of-the-art lighting, sound and music including professional DJs and bartenders.

Other Services Include

- Custom made menus catering to specific needs, tastes and dietary requirements
- An exquisite collection of crockery, cutlery, linen and glassware
- World cuisines prepared by specialty master chefs
- Resourceful and well-trained staff for service.
- Sophisticated communication network
- A state-of-the-art and vast range of kitchen and service equipment
- Transportation fleet
- Hospitality professionals that care for your image.

Scope of Services

Our team works closely with professionals in other disciplines including accountants, architects, planners, surveyors, construction companies and consulting engineers on major assignments both at the macro and micro levels either as the lead consultants or as part of a multi-disciplinary team.

Our Scope of Services Include

- Conceptualization of the project
- Construction project management
- Operational management systems
- New restaurant start-up
- Food Service Consulting
- Culinary consulting
- Performance analysis
- Management and staff training
- Hands-on Instruction
- Operational efficiency Review
- Business plans
- Restaurant and kitchen design,facility management with proper layout and equipment selection including maintenance schedules
- Menu implementation: Standardized recipes, training of restaurant and kitchen staff
- Vendor selection; sourcing products at optimum prices while maintaining quality
- Receiving , maintaining inventory and implementation
- Sales and marketing
- Maintaining International food safety and hygiene standards with HACCP control
- Computer systems and software planning; determining business needs and training
- Human resources : Job descriptions, standing orders, statuary obligations , HR policies and procedures
- Loss and fire prevention, fire safety measures , fire fighting training , fire drills

- Quality assurance and total quality management benchmarked to international standards
- Guest Relations
- Profit enhancement
- Productivity improvement

Hospitality Law Event to Examine Privacy

A host of legal trends affecting the hospitality industry will be put under the microscope at this year's Hospitality Law Conference. The conference, presented by HospitalityLawyer.com, takes place 9 February to 11 February at the Omni Houston. The event is expected to attract approximately 300 attorneys, risk managers, human resource officials and C-level executives, said Stephen Barth, founder of HospitalityLawyer.com and professor of hospitality law and leadership at the University of Houston.

"There's a lot of value for the attendees," he said. "I also hope they walk away with new relationships." He added, "Our goal is to bring them up to speed on everything that has happened in the past 12 months. Issues under discussion during the event will include health care, privacy and security, joint ventures, franchising and more, Barth said. Following is a preview of a few additional topics of discussion on the conference's agenda.

Media Strategy

Christian Stegmaier, an attorney at Collins & Lacy, is scheduled to be part of a panel that will look at what hoteliers can learn from some of the news stories that arose from the hospitality industry during the past year. Some of the more intense coverage surrounded the outbreak of bedbugs at several hotel properties. Because bedbugs are associated with a lack of cleanliness, hoteliers should do everything in their power to keep the bedbug problem quiet while addressing the issue.

"No comment is no answer," Stegmaier said. Be sure to get the message out that the existence of bedbugs does not mean the hotel is dirty; rather, the little pests are more a product of an increasing amount of international travel. In fact, Stegmaier said when dealing with the media, it is best to be aggressive and own the message. Respond quickly while being cordial and honest. "The bottom line is if something comes up, whether it's through Twitter, YouTube, the TV or newspapers, you have to be proactive," he said.

PCI Compliance

Data security also is going to be a major focus at this year's Hospitality Law Conference. Stephen Cannon, chairman of Constantine Cannon and managing partner of the firm's Washington, D.C. office, will advocate for a more equitable way of assigning liability when data security issues arise. Right now, liability is on the merchants' side of things but not on the payment systems, and that has to change, said Cannon, who is counsel to the Merchants Payment Coalition.

"Right now, all liability runs downhill and at the bottom is the merchants' coalition and, partially, the hospitality industry," he said. Cannon added he would like to see more incentives put in place to encourage more secure methods of payment authorization. One example of this is the "chip and PIN" system in use outside of the United States. In this system, credit cards use a tiny PIN-activated microchip that protects payment information.

"As it stands, virtually every Western and Eastern nation have migrated to this (system)," Cannon said. "You know which countries haven't? Iran and the U.S." The federal government is reviewing the issue of data security liability and could potentially come up with a new way of assigning liability by 21 July of this year.

HR in Hospitality

The only event specifically for HR, employment law and labor relations professionals within the hospitality industry. Produced in association with Human Resource Executive® magazine, Cornell University School of Hotel Administration,

Center for Hospitality Research and ILR School this conference delivers sessions developed by experts and senior executives – so you get cutting-edge, practical advice that you can put into action immediately. At this unique event you'll get specific strategies and solutions to help you take on today's unique operational and regulatory challenges within the hospitality sector. Additionally, the conference's Expo Hall features leading vendors of HR hospitality products and services as well as numerous networking opportunities.

Los Angeles Times Travel & Adventure Show

Los Angeles Times Travel & Adventure Show (www.latimes.com/travelshow), the nation's largest consumer travel expo, will transform the L.A. Convention Center into a world of discovery on March 19th and 20th, bringing together industry authorities, hundreds of exhibitors and thousands of adventurers. Arthur Frommer, Huell Howser, Andrew McCarthy and Rick Steves will headline the two-day exhibition, packed with expert advice, topical panel discussions and destination workshops. In addition to getting insider tips and recommendations, attendees can browse the five-acre show floor for their next adventure — from the most thrilling to the most chill locations around the globe.

"Travel is about escaping the confines of everyday life, and it's also about becoming a citizen of the world — embracing new ideas and perspectives," said Catharine Hamm, Los Angeles Times Travel Editor. "This year, we're particularly excited to welcome Andrew McCarthy, who embodies that notion, along with the industry's most experienced travelers who will help attendees identify where to go, what to do and how to save money."

McCarthy, widely known as an actor with roles in pop culture phenomena "Pretty in Pink" and "Gossip Girl," is also an accomplished travel journalist who's making his first appearance at the Los Angeles Times Travel & Adventure Show. He has won two Lowell Thomas Awards, is a contributing editor at *National Geographic Traveler*, and has written for *Travel+Leisure, Men's Journal, The Atlantic* and *Slate*. Frommer, a long-time show participant, is recognized for his best-selling guidebook series featuring more than 340 titles covering every major destination in the world, as well as a nationally-syndicated column and weekly radio program. Beloved and respected, television personality Howser is known for his critically-acclaimed PBS series "California's Gold," "Visiting with Huell Howser," and "Downtown." Steves is an authority on trans-Atlantic travel that has written more than 30 books and hosts the long-running public television series "Rick Steves' Europe" as well as a weekly radio program.

Los Angeles Times Travel staff writers, special correspondents and favorite sources will also appear throughout the weekend. Presentations, panels and workshops will address various aspects of travel, locations near and far, and a range of appetites for adventure. Sessions will also provide practical information on how to find the best deals, choose the right itinerary and more.

Los Angeles Times Travel & Adventure Show's Presenting Sponsor is the Automobile Club of Southern California. Taiwan is the Major Sponsor and KTLA is the Media Sponsor. The event, co-produced by Unicomm, LLC and the Los Angeles Times, will take place at the L.A. Convention Center Saturday, March 19th and Sunday, March 20th, 2011, 10:00 a.m. to 5:00 p.m.; trade hours 8:00 to 10:00 a.m. on Saturday. Tickets are $12 at the door or $9 online in advance (promo code "LAPR"); one child age 16 and below admitted free with paid adult.

Pennsylvania Gaming Congress & Mid-Atlantic Racing Forum

Fox Rothschild LLP, a Philadelphia-based law firm with one of the largest gaming practices in the United States, returns as Presenting Sponsor of the Pennsylvania Gaming Congress & Mid-Atlantic Racing Forum.

"As one of the region's largest gaming law practices, Fox Rothschild is proud to sponsor the Pennsylvania Gaming

Congress," said Marie J. Jones, a partner in the firm's Gaming Law practice. "We're particularly delighted Philadelphia was chosen as the venue for this year's conference. The city is a terrific location, not only because it offers a wealth of history and culture for conference attendees to enjoy but also because of many issues involving the gaming industry as it strives to sustain its success are connected to Philadelphia."

The Pennsylvania Gaming Congress & Mid-Atlantic Racing Forum annually attracts 300-plus attendees, including casino operators, developers, vendors, attorneys, investors, analysts, public officials, architects, designers and other industry-related professionals. This year's event will include three prominent keynote speakers and two intensive days of panel discussions, as well as an evening cocktail reception and outstanding networking opportunities. Among the panels on the program for the 2011 event:

- Racing Industry Trends and Updates — The latest developments and outlook for racing in the Mid-Atlantic.
- Racing and Gaming: Chasing the Synergies — What racinos are doing to encourage crossover play between casino gamblers and horse players.
- All Busy on the Western Front — Casino operators discuss the $1.3 billion western Pennsylvania and northern West Virginia gaming market.
- The Candid View from Wall Street — A no-holds-barred discussion of Pennsylvania gaming by five of the most respected gaming-industry analysts.
- Key Developments in the Keystone State — A potpourri panel covering the late-breaking gaming issues in Pennsylvania.
- The Beast in the East — Casino operators from the Poconos to Philadelphia examine the intensely competitive Eastern Pennsylvania gaming market.
- Legislative and Regulatory Update — Legislators, public officials and regulators discuss developments

in Harrisburg that could further shape the gaming industry.

The Pennsylvania Gaming Congress & Mid-Atlantic Racing Forum is organized and produced by Spectrum Gaming Group, the foremost independent research and professional services firm serving private- and public-sector clients worldwide. The firm's services include comprehensive feasibility studies and economic impact reports. Spectrum also publishes the Gaming Industry Observer newsletter and produces three other leading conferences: East Coast Gaming Congress, Florida Gaming Summit and New England Gaming Summit.

Alimentaria&Horexpo Lisboa 2011

For the first time, one exhibition will bring together in one venue the whole offer of Food & Drinks, Food service and Hospitality, and Food & Drinks Technology.

The show has born from the fusion of the two most important fairs in their respective sectors in Portugal: Alimentaria Lisboa and Horexpo.

The simultaneous celebration of both fairs will allow the visitor to access to a large range of products in the same venue. THREE SHOWS IN ONE: Alimentaria, Horexpo and Tecnoalimentaria.

The Show gives visitors the opportunity to know the Portuguese market and its products in detail. This is the only trade fair in the world where visitors can access to such wide and varied offer of Portuguese products: food and beverages, equipment for hotels, restaurants and stores and technology for the manufacturing and packaging process.

Additionally, the show will present a wide range of products of international companies from numerous countries, such as Germany, United Kingdom, Bulgaria and Romania, among others, which will launch their novelties in the Portuguese market.

CHC Safety & Quality Summit

The CHC Safety & Quality Summit is an internationally recognized aviation safety conference aimed at improving safety in aviation globally through excellence in human factors. The Summit, which will be held at the exclusive Westin Bayshore Resort & Marina in Vancouver, B.C., Canada, March 28 – 30, 2011, will open its early bird registration beginning December 13, 2010.

Remember to register now at the early bird price of $849 CAD plus tax, only available until January 6, 2011. That's a $100 savings off the regular price of $949 CAD plus tax.

Early bird registration for the Summit can be completed by visiting the Summit's website, www. chcsafety quality summit .com, following the link located on the right-hand side of the web page.

The Summit attracts the brightest experts from around the globe to share best practices and explore the latest in safety management systems, human factors of safety, and creating a safety culture.

This year's Summit, under the theme of Corporate Responsibility vs. Personal Accountability: *Two Sides of the Same Coin,* will feature 40 sessions for participants to choose from, presented by an impressive array of experts.

The annual, non-profit Summit is hosted by CHC, one of the world's largest providers of helicopter services to search and rescue and to the global offshore oil gas industry, with aircraft operating in more than 30 countries worldwide.

International Hotel Technology Forum (IHTF) 2010

The International Hotel Technology Forum (IHTF) is the leading face-to-face event for the hotel technology industry. IHTF offers blanket effectiveness, enabling senior executives from leading international hotel groups to do business with influential supplier companies. Alongside the one-to-one meetings there will run a conference programme, led by industry experts, will include topics such as 'Biometrics and

Hotel Infrastructure' as well as a panel discussion; 'Fifty minutes to have your say and listen to what's hot and what's not within the hotel industry'. In addition there will be other workshops and presentations as well as case studies throughout the event.

Corporate Sports Hospitality & Travel Packages

At EB Corporate, we identify and evaluate our clients' needs and expectations. We develop a sports-marketing initiative that accommodates budgets with aggressive pricing and customize it to your group size to produce events tailored to maximize satisfaction and return-on-investment.

EB Corporate's programs can offer great, hard to get seats, celebrity guests, haute cuisine catering, entrance into the most exclusive parties, eye-opening and classy corporate gifts, whatever is necessary to ensure your clients receive the most memorable experience possible. We strive to be your one-stop solution to all of your corporate hospitality needs.

Hotel Technology Event to Feature

Hundreds of the hospitality industry's top technology executives will gather for a week of meetings designed to stimulate thought leadership, collaboration on new technology solutions, and networking. Hotel Technology Next Generation (HTNG), a trade association dedicated to fostering the development of better technology for hospitality, is holding its seventh annual North American Members' Meeting in San Diego, and numerous more focused meetings, the week of February 28 through March 4.

As an organization run by hotel CIOs for the benefit of hotels, HTNG understands the issues that face hotel IT executives. This year's planned agenda provides thought leadership presentations and panel sessions on important hospitality technology issues—future trends, hotel data security, social media/networking, sustainability, designing secure software, systems integration, and cloud computing. There will also be sessions on new HTNG developments that can be deployed by hotels and vendors and an always-popular hotel CIO panel.

HTNG's members' meetings are for members only, but in order to help hoteliers learn more about how this dynamic organization can help them, HTNG is making a special offer this year for hoteliers who are not members and who have never attended this event before. For just the cost of an individual one-year membership ($325), they can get a *free* registration for the annual meeting, and can also attend any forum and workgroup meetings. Vendors who are not yet HTNG members but who wish to attend can do so at a discount by joining HTNG and enjoying early-bird registration rates and exhibit space incentives, which have been extended exclusively for new members.

A few of the sessions are yet to be announced, but those confirmed to date include:

- ***Creating the IT-Free Hotel*** - This session will discuss La Quinta's initiative to move virtually all property-based systems above property, using cloud, SaaS and ASP models. The session will be presented by one of the many hotel CIO speakers at the event, **Vivek Shaiva**, CIO, La Quinta Inns & Suites.
- ***Messaging In the Cloud*** - Hyatt Hotels & Resorts is implementing a replacement for its corporate messaging platform with a cloud-based solution based on Microsoft's Office 365 suite. In addition to cost savings gained while providing email to all employees, Hyatt will gain reliability, agility, and eliminate the cost and support burden of software upgrades and mail servers. Hyatt CIO **Mike Blake** and **Trevor Strawhecker** from Microsoft will co-present about the Microsoft cloud solution; how it suited the Hyatt environment; and the opportunities uncovered and lessons learned through the implementation process.
- ***The Changing Face of Hotel Credit Card Breaches*** - It's no secret that hotels have been a prime target of professional credit card thieves in recent years. But

as hotels have beefed up their security efforts, so too have the thieves evolved their methods to beat them. Three of the top experts in the field, with deep forensic data on hundreds of hotel breaches, will discuss the latest data, the trends they are seeing in breaches generally and in hotels specifically, the anatomy of breaches, and how hotels can protect their data - and their reputation. They will also address the difficult issue of enforcing compliance through franchise networks. Speakers for this session include **Jennifer Fischer**, Director, Payment System Risk & Compliance, Visa USA; **Colin Sheppard**, Director of Incident Response, Trustwave; and **Steve Surdu**, VP of Professional Services, Mandiant.

- ***The Sustainable Hotel: Why and How*** - Every major hotel company has recognized the need for a sustainability program, and hotels that have adopted sustainability programs are recognizing cost savings, revenue benefits, and image improvements that result from socially responsible behavior. Technology is a key enabler for the majority of sustainability programs. **Chuck Marratt**, VP Technology for MTM Luxury Lodging, will explore how technology can be applied to achieve business benefits through sustainability. It will also discuss HTNG's ongoing role in fostering the development of cost-effective, sustainable technologies - and in making them work. This session is still evolving and additional speaker(s) may be added.
- ***Case Studies of HTNG Implementations*** - With a number of HTNG specifications now reaching full maturity and widespread adoption, hotel companies are now building hotels with more and more HTNG-designed capabilities built in. What have the challenges been, and what are the benefits to the hotels and their preferred vendors? This session will highlight some implementations with perspectives from both hoteliers and vendors. The session will be led by **Jim Peterson,** Senior Vice President of Enterprise Architecture for

Marriott International, and will include participation from a number of vendors who have participated in high-profile projects.

The event will be held at the beautiful Rancho Bernardo Inn in San Diego, CA. The main meeting starts Tuesday evening, March 1 with a welcome reception for all attendees, and continues through Thursday with general sessions. For details, review this list of speakers and the general session agenda on HTNG's website.

On Monday and Tuesday, HTNG's Infrastructure and Device Forum, its Software Forum, and about ten separate working groups, will hold face-to-face meetings to further their collaborative efforts on topics as diverse as entertainment system content, back office system integration, cellular coverage, network infrastructure, telephony, distribution, guest device connectivity, and other topics.

The second awarding of the Most Innovative Hospitality Technology will be announced on Thursday afternoon. Seventeen contenders are vying for the title this year, to be voted on by HTNG's hotelier and consultant members. A fun golf outing will wrap up the week on Friday morning.

8

GLOBAL HOTEL CHAINS

Climate Counts, a nonprofit that scores the world's largest companies on efforts to shrink their carbon footprint, has released its latest ranking of major hotel companies—and once again this year, Marriott heads the pack. Six hoteliers–Marriott, Hyatt, Hilton, Starwood, Wyndham and Carlson—were included in the annually updated scorecard. The companies self-report their efforts in 22 areas, including support for climate legislation and a clear, complete articulation of their climate action strategies.

Based on a point scale of 0 to 100, Marriott finished highest with a score of 62, followed by Starwood with 38, Hyatt with 29, Wyndham with 27, Hilton with 23, and Carlson with 13. All the companies but Hilton bettered their scores over the previous year.

Concludes Climate Counts, "The world's largest hotel chains may be seeking practical ways to address a range of broad environmental impacts in their operations, from toxic chemical use to indoor air quality to water. However, few appear to be aligning such actions as part of a larger and more comprehensive carbon management strategy. An average sector score of 19 out of a possible 100 suggests the sector has much work ahead."

HOTEL CHAINS IN INDIA

India is an incredible tourist destination. Visitors to India are enchanted by the richness of its culture, touched by the warmth of its people, amazed by the grandeur of its monuments and delighted by the excellent standards of its hotels.There are numerous hotel chains in india. India for You highlights some of the leading hotel chains of India. These India hotels chains is renowned and some less frequented tourist destinations, offer world-class services, as well as traditional Indian hospitality. Some of the leading international hotel chains have their properties housed across major cities in India. These hotels in India enables you to experience the same standards of service that you can expect in any leading hotel in the world, along with India's unique charm.

Stay in the hotels of the leading hotel chains of India and you're sure to have a pleasant and memorable stay. Whether it's a luxurious palace hotel or a serene wildlife resort, hotel chains in India offer an ideal place to rest and relax before you head out for another days adventure, exploring the wonders of India.

BEST HOTEL CHAINS IN INDIA

Mentioned below are the significant *hotel chains of India,* which is waiting to be your host while on tour to India.

Taj Group of Hotels in India

The most popular name that is almost synonymous to hospitality in India is that of the Taj Group. Offering the best hotels across various genres like business hotels, heritage resorts, luxury hotels and even sea resorts, the Taj Group is definitely the best in the field.

The Oberoi Group of Hotels in India

One of the most prominent names among the hotel chains of India is the Oberoi Group. It also owns several properties in exotic places like Australia and Mauritius. With its world class facilities and efficient staff to manage and play the perfect Indian hosts, the Oberoi hotels is no doubt a great feather on the grand cap of tourism in India.

Le Meridien Group of Hotels

The Le Meridien Group of Hotels has played an instrumental role in playing the perfect host to the millions of tourists and guests coming here. It is a luxury brand of great fame and reflects the inherent Le Meridien touch of elegance and class through all its properties in India. It is no wonder one of the exclusive hotel chains of India.

Best Western Group

A world famous name when it comes to hospitality and service, the Best Western Group owns several properties across India. Each of the hotels has been equipped with numerous features to enable a cozy comfortable stay to the guest. Browse through the pages of Indfy.com to know about the properties and amenities offered in the hotels of Best Western Group.

List of The Best Groups of Hotel Chains in India

- Best Western Group
- Park Group of Hotels
- Sangam Group of Hotels
- Grand Intercontinental Group
- Elgin Group of Heritage Hotels
- Kenilworth Group of Hotels
- Hindusthan Group of Hotels
- Days Inn Hotels in India
- Four Points Hotels in India
- Fortune Hotels in India
- Hyatt Group of Hotels
- ITC Group of Hotels
- Marriott Group of Hotels
- Ramada Group of Hotels Hotels
- Sinclairs Group of Hotels
- Choice Group of Hotels

- Neemrana Group of Hotels
- Le Meridien Group of Hotels
- The ITDC Ashok Group of Hotels
- Taj Group of Hotels
- The Oberoi Group Hotels in India
- Holiday Inn Hotels in India
- Four Seasons Hotels in India
- HRH Group of Hotels
- Jaypee Group of Hotels
- Leela Kempensky Hotels
- Park Plaza Group of Hotels
- Shangri La Group of Hotels
- Trident Group Of Hotels

HOTEL CHAINS IN THE UNITED KINGDOM

Britannia Hotels

Britannia Hotels is a UK based hotel company with 36 hotels across the country. Britannia generally operate at the budget end of the market, with hotels varying in price and star ratings around the country. In 2011 the company purchased the beleaguered Pontin's holiday camp chain.

Britannia Hotels started in 1976 with the purchase of a hotel in Manchester, The Britannia Country House Hotel in Didsbury. Britannia Hotels' head office is based in the old Town Hall in Hale, Manchester. A large cluster of Britannia Hotels are located in and around Manchester.

The company employs over 4,000 people. Britannia does not build hotels, instead preferring to buy existing hotels, and to refurbish and up-date them, restoring original features where possible. In some cases Britannia have taken an existing structure and converted it into a hotel.

Some hotels maintain their original name, without the addition of the word Britannia. In such cases, flags displaying the Britannia Hotels logo and name are erected outside.

Britannia Hotels make extensive use of email in its operations. Senior hotel staff members are provided with their own addresses, departments have their own address, hotels have several addresses and contact can only be made through email on the company's website. Bookings can be made through email as well as online or phone. Each hotel is assigned a three digit number, in front of which, the word 'res' is placed. This allows bookings to be sent straight to the reservations department. A similar process is used to send enquiries direct to hotel reception desks, banqueting departments etc.

Rooms

Britannia Hotels do not all have a common theme or look, each hotel being somewhat individual. Bedrooms have different furnishings in each hotel, although rooms recently refurbished are generally in the same style. Even though the company operates in the budget sector, upscale features such Jacuzzi Baths, trouser presses, room service and balconies are found in a number of their hotels.

Events

In the mid-1980s, Alex Langsam, owner of the Britannia Hotel Group, acquired the Grade II* listed London Road Fire Station in Manchester. There have been a series of proposals made to redevelop the facility into a hotel and office, however the plans have been delayed and postponed. The City of Manchester has taken an interest in taking control of the redevelopment process. In 2006 it was placed on English Heritage's register of "at risk" historical buildings.

In 2004, Grand Hotels Group sold their four resort hotels to Britannia Hotels. These hotels are undergoing extensive refurbishment, with millions of pounds being spent to restore them. These Hotels offer Entertainment Breaks, with live entertainment each evening in the Ballrooms.

In 2006, Britannia celebrated their 30th anniversary by adding their 30th Hotel (Britannia Bournemouth) to the chain, this number has later risen to 36 UK properties.

In 2007, many properties have undergone refurbishment, including the Britannia Manchester, and the Adelphi Hotel in Liverpool.

In 2008 as part of the Capital of Culture celebrations a musical has been written based on the Adelphi Hotel in Liverpool. Written and directed by Phil Willmott, Once Upon A Time At The Adelphi ran at the Liverpool Playhouse from 30 June and after an extension closed on 2 August.

Champneys

Champneys is the brand name of the largest destination spa group in the United Kingdom. Champneys Health Resorts Group currently own four spa resorts and has become one of the largest destination spa operators in the world. In 2004, Champneys launched a range of spa products called the Champneys Collection. The companies are currently owned by mother and son, Dorothy and Stephen Purdew.

orothy Purdew set up her own slimming club business and opened her first club on 25 June 1970 at Frimleys, Northampton. It was a success and led to over 70 clubs opening throughout the South East. In September 1981 the Purdew family (Dorothy and her husband Robert) purchased Henlow Grange and one of their sons Stephen joined the company. Following the death of Robert Purdew, Stephen now manages the entire group.

In 1990 they purchased Springs Health Farm in Leicestershire and invested £10 million and this was followed by a purchase of a health farm at Forest Mere in 1995. The Hotel de la Paix in Champery, Switzerland was purchased in 1996. In 2002, Henlow Grange suffered a fire however this was seen as an opportunity to undertake a multi-million pound transformation of the resort. To complete their spa portfolio, the Purdews acquired Champneys Tring, which with the Champneys name, led to the re-branding of all the resorts. The Champneys name originated from Ralph de Champneys who owned the Tring mansion in 1307. It was later opened as the UK's first ever health farm in 1925 by naturopath Stanley Lieff, who pioneered the concept of holistic health and naturopathy, along with his business partner and financial backer Edwin Herrin, a London-based solicitor whose second home was in Tring.

Resorts

The chain has four resorts in the United Kingdom:

- Champneys Henlow Grange, Henlow, Bedfordshire
- Champneys Forest Mere, Liphook, Hampshire
- Champneys Springs, Ashby-de-la-Zouch, Leicestershire
- Champneys Tring, Wigginton, Hertfordshire

The company also owns the Hotel de la Paix, a ski hotel in Champéry, Switzerland.

Town and City Spas

In 2006, Champneys opened their first high street spa in Chichester. Champneys Town and City Spas have now opened in 6 other locations including Enfield, Guildford, Tunbridge Wells, St. Albans, Brighton and Bath. The company also owns the Hotel de la Paix, a ski hotel in Champéry, Switzerland.

Easy Group

EasyGroup (styled as **easyGroup**), founded in 1998, is a conglomerate & the holding company controlling the "easy" ventures; it is privately owned by Stelios Haji-Ioannou. Many of the companies follow the "easy" format of taking away the frills in something to make it cheaper overall, plus using the yield management system of supply and demand. In the last few years the company has started to franchise the businesses to expand, and cut down costs. Its head office is in Mayfair, City of Westminster, London, although it is registered in Jersey. Some EasyGroup subsidiaries have been more successful than others - the most successful division being EasyJet.

EasyGroup Brands

EasyJet

EasyJet is a low-cost airline which commenced operations on 10 November 1995. It is one of the two largest budget airlines in Europe, alongside its sometimes bitter rival Ryanair. It was the first company owned by EasyGroup to use the "easy" prefix. EasyJet Airline Company Limited is a separate company in its own right, merely licensing the "easyJet" name from easyGroup.

EasyInternetcafé

EasyInternetcafé (formerly EasyEverything) is Europe's largest chain of Internet cafés, launched in 1999.

EasyCar.com

In April 2000 the company set-up the car rental company EasyRentacar (later renamed EasyCar), with the only rental car available being the Mercedes-Benz A-Class. The car rental business, which suffered from financial losses and a reputation for poor service has since closed. The new EasyCar company now operates as an international car rental broker via the Internet. The business is profitable and operates in more than 2,400 locations in over 60 countries, selling a full fleet of vehicles, including Prestige Cars in the UK.

EasyMoney

On 21 August 2001 the credit card company, EasyMoney was set up with Accucard (now part of Lloyds TSB), which was expanded on 14 February 2005 with the announcement that unbundled car insurance products provided by Zurich would be sold later in the year at EasyMoney insurance . In April 2006, EasyGroup linked with Moneysupermarket.com to provide a financial product comparison website. This coincided with the withdrawal of the EasyMoney credit card.

EasyCinema

On 23 May 2003 the cinema company, EasyCinema at The

Point, Milton Keynes was opened at a former UCI site, offering screenings from 20p if booked well in advance. The cinema initially struggled as major distributors were not prepared to release new films to the company using the yield-management model.

First run films later became available, but at fixed prices. The cinema also relented on not serving popcorn and drinks, which previously went unsold to save on staffing costs.

Towards the end of its life, the cinema site also housed an EasyInternetcafé and was a pick-up point for EasyPizza. However, following a dispute over unpaid rent with the landlord, Odeon, which resulted in eviction, the EasyCinema closed in May 2006 and reopened as an Odeon cinema.

The closure of EasyCinema appears to have curtailed the desired expansion into London's West End.

EasyCinema DVD Rental

10 March 2005 saw the commencement of EasyCinema DVD Rental, first announced in November 2004. This is a partnership with LoveFilm, the company operating rental services for several other retail brands. However, unlike many online DVD rental services, there is no monthly subscription but the user purchases credits at £1.99 each (minimum purchase is 4 credits). One credit permits one DVD rental and a maximum of three DVDs can be rented at one time, depending on how many credits are pre-purchased. For customers renting one disc per week the offering is competitive to the subscription services, which typically allow one rental at a time, charging around £7.97 to £9.99 per month.

EasyBus

EasyBus began operating on 30 July 2004. The company currently offers a low-cost express minibus service between Central London and three London airports: Gatwick, Stansted and Luton. Journeys can be booked via the EasyBus website, or customers can purchase, usually at higher prices, from the EasyBus airport sales desks, or by paying the driver if joining in London. Online bookings offer guaranteed seats on specific services.

Easy4Men

On 9 December 2004 the men's toiletries range Easy4Men was launched together with Boots. Originally conceived to challenge Gillette, the product line did not include a razor. After disappointing sales the partnership with Boots was dissolved in 2006.

EasyPizza

A delivery-only pizza company launched in 2004.

EasyMusic

EasyMusic, in conjunction with Wippit, began operation on 22 December 2004, with copyrighted music downloads offered from 25p, although minimum transaction value is £1 and there are charges for using credit cards and SMS payment methods. A proposed copyleft section of EasyMusic never materialised.

As of January 2008, EasyMusic no longer sells download music, but sells CDs in conjunction with CD-WOW.COM. When purchasing a CD, customers are diverted to the CD-WOW website and a discount is usually applied which varies depending on purchase, most transactions cost around 15p.

EasyCruise

A no frills cruise ship targeting the 18-40 age-group, rather than the traditional retired market, was launched on Friday 6 May 2005. The first vessel was known as *EasyCruiseOne*. Expansion of the EasyCruise fleet was announced in 2006. A franchise operation using a converted river freighter *EasyCruiseTwo* operated from 2006 until August 17, 2007. A third ship, a converted ferry, *EasyCruise Life* was purchased and began service in May 2008. *EasyCruiseOne* was sold in late 2008. The EasyCruiseOne cabins offered a simple bed and bathroom: most did not originally have windows and use of a maid service during the stay incurred an additional charge. Stelios revealed that the initial idea of requiring customers to be responsible for all room cleaning or incur a penalty charge "didn't go down too well". EasyCruise, based in Liberia, was a wholly owned subsidiary of EasyGroup, managed by V Ships of Monaco until sold to Hellenic Seaways in August 2009 for £9 million. The launch and early days of EasyCruise were tracked for a three series Sky One programme *Cruise with Stelios.*

EasyMobile/ShimmerBright

EasyMobile was a mobile virtual network operator, operating a pay as you go service, which closed in 2006 following a string of negative publicity and the withdrawal of its principal backer, TDC.

Rival mobile service, Orange, attempted to sue EasyGroup as it claimed the use of the orange EasyMobile logo breached its trademark and could confuse customers. EasyGroup challenged this assertion. The EasyMobile operation was inspired by Telmore, a Danish mobile virtual network operator, using the TDC Mobil network.

EasyMobile chose The Link to be its sole independent retailer in March 2006, adding UK electrical retailer Comet to its vendors in May 2006. In April 2005, it was announced EasyMobile would expand into the Netherlands by summer 2005 in partnership with Telfort. Nine months after launch the operation ceased on 1 August 2006 and the EasyMobile.nl website would be transformed into a telecoms price-comparison engine in partnership with Kelkoo. In September 2005 it was announced that the service would also launch in Germany in partnership with T-Mobile . On 10 November 2006 Talkline Gmbh & Co. KG, a German subsidiary of TDC Mobile International, bought 100% of EasyMobile Germany and EasyMobile Germany was renamed Callmobile. The MNVO Callmobile is still operated by Talkline.

On November 10, 2006 the EasyGroup terminated the brand license for EasyMobile. All customers were offered transfers to fresh mobile or a PAC to join another network. The network closed on 13 December at midnight and the Easymobile.com website was transformed into a telecoms price-comparison engine. EasyMobile was temporarily called ShimmerBright in the UK before it was shut down permanently in February 2007.

In January, 2008 the EasyGroup launched a partnership with the Mobile VoIP provider Rebtel. With this service, users can make international calls for the cost of a local call from their regular mobile phone and carrier without additional software downloads, Internet connections or computers. The service leverages VoIP technology to route the international leg of the call over the Internet passing the savings on to the user.

EasyHotel

EasyHotel is a "no frills super budget" hotel operator with hotels located in South Kensington, Victoria, Paddington, Heathrow, and Earls Court, London as well as Luton, Basel, Zurich, Budapest, Sofia and Berlin. Locations for future openings in 2009 have been announced as Larnaca (summer 2009), Dubai, and in 2010, Edinburgh. Rooms contain a double bed, are en-suite and one wall panel is orange in colour with corporate logos on the wall and doors. Toiletries (except soap/ shampoo) are not supplied and the use of the TV and the housekeeping facility is at an additional charge. Reservations must be made online, with the price less expensive the further in advance one books. The EasyHotel website also acts as a booking engine for 20,000 other hotels worldwide through Octopus Travel.

Other Businesses

- **EasyValue** - An internet shopping comparison site began trading in November 2000, first independently, using software from Autonomy, then later in partnership with Kelkoo, switching to Shopping.com following Yahoo's acquisition of Kelkoo.

- **Easy.com** - A free e-mail service began in November 2000. This site now also acts as the easyGroup main portal
- **EasyJobs** – An employment search engine, a partnership with JobSite.co.uk
- **EasyWatch** - A Swatch-style range of watches made by Zeon. On launching EasyWatch Stelios claimed to be filling the void left by the highly collectable Swatch brand. EasyWatches are typically orange and have a large EasyWatch logo prominently displayed, which watch collectors say makes them look like a free corporate giveaway rather than a desirable or collectable product. EasyWatch immediately managed to infringe a number of trademarks by giving its watches names like Portafino. Stelios claimed that no-one could confuse one of his watches with a genuine Portafino and expressed surprise that a company would take legal action for use of a registered trademark.
- **EasyTelecom** – Providing mobile phone comparisons powered by Kelkoo. Fills the gap left by EasyMobile.
- **EasyVan** – Like EasyCar, EasyVan.com has teamed up with an outside company (Northgate) and two other suppliers to provide van rental across the UK. EasyVan provide van hire from more than 120 locations throughout the United Kingdom, including van hire in England, Wales, Scotland and Northern Ireland.
- **EasyOffice** – owned and operated by the EasyGroup, opened in Kensington High Street in London on 14 November 2007 and is taking bookings.

Exclusive Hotels

Exclusive Hotels are a hotel chain based in Surrey, England. The hotel group has a portfolio of several hotels across the south, and operates mainly in the five star sector. The hotel group has owned Pennyhill Park Hotel in Surrey since 1982. A year later, Lainston House Hotel in Hampshire joined the group property collection. South Lodge Hotel in West Sussex was purchased in July 1985, after the last of the descendants of the original owner, Frederick DuCane Godman, died.

The hotel group also owns Manor House Hotel in Wiltshire, and Mannings Heath Golf Club in Sussex. The properties in the group collection employ a number of high-profile chefs, including the Michelin starred Chefs Michael Wignall (who has participated in television shows such as Great British Menu during his time with the group) and Richard Davies. The hotel group's Managing Director, Danny Pecorelli, has stated that the group's emphasis on fine food and luxury dining is to counter against "very mediocre restaurant offers" available in many hotels.

In recent years, the hotel group has launched the 'Exclusively Green' project, which researches, reviews and trials methods to reduce the environmental impact of the hotel group's activties e.g. for reducing the group's carbon footprint. The hotel group is also actively involved in local fund-raising events and is one of the official sponsors of MacMaillan Cancer Support.

Guoman Hotels

Guoman Hotels Ltd. is a British company operating in the hospitality industry. They currently have thirty-eight hotels (2008) within the United Kingdom and its headquarters is situated in Longford, West Drayton, sharing the same compound as the Thistle London Heathrow , a 264-bedroom hotel. It is the parent company of both the Thistle brand and the Guoman Collection of Hotels. The Thistle brand operates throughout the United Kingdom, while Guoman has four hotels under its collective branding.

Hotel du Vin

Hotel du Vin is a luxury boutique and hotel chain in the United Kingdom, co-founded by Gerard Basset and Robin

Hutson.The hotel chain was founded in Winchester in 1994 by Gerard Basset and Robin Hutson who both previously had worked at the famous Chewton Glen hotel where Basset was the Head Sommelier and Hutson the Managing Director. The name "Hotel du Vin" was a reference to Basset's wine expertise. At the time Basset was a Master Sommelier, he went on to become a Master of Wine (1998). Subsequent hotels were established in Tunbridge Wells, Bristol, Birmingham, Brighton, and Harrogate. The chain grew to six hotels before selling to MWB Group in October 2004. Gerard Basset has since gone on to become owner with his wife, Nina, of Hotel Terravina, a New Forest Hotel near Southampton in Hampshire, United Kingdom.

MWB Group Holdings still owns Hotel du Vin as well as the Malmaison hotel chain, the Liberty store in London and MWB Business Exchange PLC an office provider. Richard Balfour-Lynn is a major share holder and the Chief Executive of the MWB company. Robert Cook is CEO of Hotel du Vin and Malmaison. After MWB purchased Hotel du Vin, the company increased the size of the group by opening new Hotel du Vins in Henley, Cheltenham, Glasgow, York, Cambridge, Newcastle, Poole and Edinburgh. The Hotel du Vin group now operates fourteen hotels across the UK in university and cathedral towns and cities.

The latest incarnation of the du Vin brand will be a Bistro du Vin sub-brand, which opens in London Early 2011, bringing the same passion for food and wine as the Hotel du Vin brand.

Macdonald Hotels

Macdonald Hotels Ltd is a hospitality company based in Bathgate, West Lothian, Scotland. Its main subsidiary, Macdonald Hotels and Resorts, owns or operates hotels and holiday resorts in the UK and Spain. Macdonald Hotels was bought from shareholders by its management in 2003 in a management buyout facilitated by Bank of Scotland The value of the transaction was £590 million It expanded rapidly with the purchase of some "Forte Heritage Hotels" from Forte

Hotels after the latter's takeover by Granada plc. In 2007 the company sold 24 hotels to Moorfield Real Estate Fund It subsequently bid for the Management Contract to continue running these hotels but lost out to Accor Hotels.

Malmaison

Malmaison is a hotel brand in the United Kingdom. The group operates 12 hotels and is wholly owned by MWB Group Holdings. The hotel brand was formed in 1994 and is named after the Château de Malmaison on the outskirts of Paris. The chain is owned by MWB Group Holdings. Their brand premise is "Hotels that dare to be different" The group also owns the Hotel du Vin hotel brand. Malmaison had a turnover of £60.271 million in 2009.There are 12 hotels located in Aberdeen, Belfast, Birmingham, Edinburgh, Glasgow, Leeds, Liverpool, London, Manchester, Newcastle upon Tyne, Oxford and Reading. Each hotel has its own website; these can be accessed by the main Malmaison hotel website.

McMillan Hotels

McMillan Hotels are a hotel chain based in Stranraer, Scotland. The hotel group has a portfolio of 6 hotels across Scotland, operating in the three, four and five star sector. The hotel group was initially created after hotelier Hammy McMillan decided to renovate the North West Castle in his hometown of Stranraer in 1961.It later became the first hotel in the world with an indoor curling ice rink , and Hammy McMillan's son of the same name would later become a World Champion curler based on his extensive practice there. Today, the hotel group continues to be owned and run by the McMillan family, who have actively spoken up on local planning issues which affect the tourism industry in the south-west of Scotland. The hotel group is actively involved in local events, particularly those of a sporting nature.

The group consists of hotels across the south-west of Scotland. Expanding most significantly during the 1990s, the group extended beyond its traditional west-coast heartland with the purchase of two hotels in Peebles in the Scottish

Borders at the end of 2004. More specifically, the hotel group's portfolio includes hotels in Dumfries and Galloway, such as the 18th century home of home of Sir John Ross, North West Castle, now serving as the group's administrative base, as well as the 'Category A' listed building Cally Palace, which was acquired in 1981. The group also has a hotel in nearby Ayrshire, the Scottish Baronial-styled Glenapp Castle. The two hotels in the Scottish Borders include the Peebles Hydro, designed by renowned Scottish architect James Miller.

Peel Hotels

Peel Hotels plc is a hotel company operating in the United Kingdom. It operates eight hotels and is listed on the AIM. The company was founded in 1998 by Robert Peel, when he bought the Bull Hotel in Peterborough. Since that date, the company has acquired other notable hotels, such as the famous Midland Railway Hotel in Bradford, and the King Malcolm Hotel in Dunfermline.

Recently the company has demised a 25 year lease to Clermont Leisure, owners of the prestigious Clermont Club casino in London, to open a casino in the basement of the Midland Hotel, taking advantage of the Gambling Act 2005 permitting new casino-hotels. The new hotel will be called the Guoman Club and will be the third casino in the city, which will effectively join the new Westfield Shopping Centre being built adjacent to the hotel. This lease, together with the recent disposal of land to the north of the Midland site to developers and the disposal of the Avon Gorge Hotel in Bristol, has left the hotel group debt-free.

GLOBAL HOTEL CHAINS

- Abba Hoteles
- AC HOTELS
- Acc-Nifos Hotels
- ACCOR Hotels
- Active Hotels
-

- Adagio City Aparthotel
- Affinia Hospitality
- All Seasons Europe
- Aloft
- AmericInn
- AmeriHost Inn Hotels
- AmeriSuites
- ANA Hotels International
- Atel Hotels
- Atlantis
- Axcess Hotels
- Banyan Tree Hotels
- Barcelo Hotels
- Barcelo Hotels UK
- Baymont Inn & Suites
- Beaches Resorts
- Best Inns and Suites
- Best Value Inn and Suites
- Best Western International
- Boscolo Hotels
- Boutique
- Boutique Desires Hotels
- Brisas Hotels & Resorts
- Bulgari Hotels
- Caesar Park Hotels & Resorts
- Cambria Suites
- Camino Real Hotels & Resorts
- Candlewood Suites
- City Partners Hotels
- Clarion

- Classic British Hotels
- Classic International Hotels
- Club Quarters
- ClubHouse Inn & Suites
- Coast Hotels
- Columbus Reservation Services
- Comfort Inns
- Comfort Suites
- Concorde Hotels
- Conrad Hotels
- CORALIA CLUB - Accor vacances
- Corus Hotels
- Country Inns & Suites
- Courtyard by Marriott
- Crowne Plaza Hotels and Resorts
- Days Inn
- De Vere Hotels
- Delta Hotels
- Derag Hotels
- Design Hotels
- Destination Hotels & Resorts
- Distinguished Hotels
- Dolce International
- Domina Hotels
- Doral Hotels
- Dorchester Group Hotels
- Dorint Resorts
- Doubletree Hotels
- Drury Hotels
- Econo Lodge

- El Cid
- Element
- Embassy Suites
- Envergure Hotels
- Epoque Hotels
- Eryokan
- Exclusive Hotels
- Executive Hotels and Resorts
- Extended StayAmerica
- Extra Holidays
- Fairfield Inn by Marriott
- Fairmont Hotels
- Fiesta Americana Hotels & Resorts
- First Hotels
- Flag Hotels
- Four Points by Sheraton
- Gaylord Entertainment
- GenaRes Worldwide Reservation Services
- Global Conextions
- Global Hotel Alliance
- GlobRes
- Golden Tulip
- Grand Heritage Hotels
- Grand Hospitality
- Grand Pineapple Beach Resorts
- Grange Hotels
- Great Hotels of the World
- GuestHouse International
- Hampton Inn/Hampton Inn and Suites
- Hard Rock Hotels

- Harrahs Entertainment
- Harvey Hotels and Suites
- Hawthorn Suites
- Hilton Garden Inn
- Hilton Hotels and Resorts (U.S.)
- Hilton International
- Historic Hotels of America
- Holiday Inn Express
- Holiday Inn Hotels and Resorts
- Homewood Suites
- Hotel AG
- Hotel Provider SRL
- Hotelbook
- HotelREZ
- Hotels and Preference
- Hotelzon International Ltd
- Hotlink Hotels
- Hotusa Hotels
- Howard Johnson Plazas, Hotels, Inns, and Express Inns
- Hyatt Hotels and Resorts
- Hyatt Vacation Club
- Ian Schrager
- IBIS - Accor hotels
- Independent Hotels
- Indigo
- InnLink Inns
- InnPoints Reserv
- InnPoints Worldwide
- Inter-Continental Hotels and Resorts

- InterCity Hotels
- Interstate Hotels and Resorts
- ITWG - Italy and world hotels
- Joie de Vivre
- Jolly Hotels
- Jumeirah
- Jumer Hotels
- Jurys Doyle Hotel Group
- Jurys Inns
- Karyon
- Kempinski Hotels & Resorts
- Kerry Hotels
- Keytel
- Kimpton Hotels
- Knights Inn
- KSL Resorts
- Langham Hotels
- Le Meridien
- Leading Hotels of the World
- LeisureLink
- Leonardo Hotels
- Lexington Collection
- Loews Hotels
- Lucien Barriere
- Luxe Worldwide Hotels
- Luxury Lifestyle Hotels and Resorts
- Luxury Resorts
- Macdonald Hotels
- Magnolia Hotels and Resorts
- MainStay Suites

- Malmaison Hotels
- Mandarin Oriental Hotel Group
- Marco Polo Hotels
- Maritim Hotels
- Marriott Conference Centers
- Marriott Hotels, Resorts, and Suites
- Marriott Vacation Club International
- Maybourne Hotel Group
- MERCURE - Accor Hotels
- Mercure Gallery
- Meritus Hotels & Resorts
- MGM Grand Hotels
- MI Independent Property
- Microtel Inns and Suites
- Millennium & Copthorne Hotels
- Moevenpick Hotels & Resorts
- Morgans Hotel Group
- Myfidelio.net
- New Otani Hotels
- NH Hotels
- Nikko Hotels International
- Noble House
- Norlandia Hotels
- Oberoi Group of Hotels
- Okura Hotels & Resorts
- Omni Hotels
- Orient-Express Hotels
- Otedis Hotels
- Outrigger Hotels Hawaii
- Pacific International

- Pan Pacific Hotels and Resorts
- Park Inn
- Park Plaza
- Performance Connections
- Preferred Hotels; and Resorts Worldwide
- Prince Hotels
- Principal Hotels
- Pullman
- Purple Hotels
- QHOTELS
- Quality Inns
- Quality Reservations
- Radisson Hotels & Resorts
- Raffles International Hotels and Resorts
- Ramada Plazas, Limiteds, and Inns
- RCI Hotels
- Reconline
- Red Carnation Hotels
- Red Lion Hotels & Inns
- Red Roof Inns
- Refad Hotels & Resorts
- Regent International Hotels
- Relais & Chateaux
- Renaissance Hotels and Resorts
- ReservHOTELs
- Residence Inn by Marriott
- Resort Bookings
- Resort Quest International
- ResortQuest Hawaii
- Rezlink

- REZOnline
- RIHGA Royal Hotels
- Ringhotels
- Ritz-Carlton Hotels
- Rocco Forte Hotels
- Rockresorts
- Rodeway Inn
- Rosewood Hotels and Resorts
- Rydges Hotels
- Sandals Resorts
- Sandman Hotels
- Sarova Hotels
- Scandic Hotels
- Sceptre
- Select Marketing Hotels
- Sercotel Hoteles Independientes
- Shangri-La Hotels and Resorts
- Sheraton Hotels and Resorts
- Shilo Resorts
- Sierra Suites Hotels
- Signature/Jameson Inns
- Six Senses Resorts & Spas
- Sleep Inns
- Small Luxury Hotels of the World
- SOFITEL - Accor Hotels and Resorts
- Sokos Hotels
- Sol Melia
- Sonesta Hotels and Resorts
- SORAT Hotels
- SpringHill Suites

- St Regis
- STARHOTELS
- Staybridge Suites by Holiday Inn
- Steigenberger
- Sterling Hotels and Resorts
- Studio 6
- Suburban Hotels
- SUITE HOTELS - Accor Hotels
- Summit Hotels and Resorts
- Super 8 Motels
- Supranational Hotels
- Swissotel
- Switzerland Travel Centre
- Synxis
- Taj Hotels, Resorts & Palaces
- The Charming Hotels of the World
- The Luxury collection
- The Peninsula Hotels
- The Sutton Place Hotels
- Thistle Hotels
- TOP International Hotels
- TownePlace Suites
- TRADYSO (TRAVEL DYNAMIC SOLUTIONS)
- TravelCLICK
- Travelodge
- Travelodge UK
- TravTech
- Trident Hotels
- Trust Hospitality
- TShotels

- Unirez
- Universal
- Univisit
- Utell
- VacationClick
- Vagabond Inns
- Vantis Hotels
- Vantis Hotels Group
- W Hotels
- Waldorf Astoria
- Warwick International Hotels
- Webres
- WestCoast Hotel Partners
- Westin Hotels and Resorts
- Wingate Inns
- Woodfin Suites
- WORLDHOTELS
- Wyndham Hotels and Resorts
- XN Corporation
- Your Hotel Worldwide

9

HOTEL INVESTMENT EVENTS

The 7th Russia & CIS Hotel Investment Conference (RHIC) will take 17 - 19 October 2011 at the Radisson Royal Hotel, Moscow. RHIC is one of the largest gatherings of hotel investors, operators and developers to focus on Russia & CIS, with over 400 hotel investors, operators, developers, advisors and country officials from the region and beyond, exploring new investment opportunities in the region.

Networking is high on the agenda and 2011 will see the return of Networking xPress, which had a fantastic turnout last year with over 100 people participating in the fast paced business card exchange. Delegates will also be treated to two evening networking receptions, one at the host hotel, the Radisson Royal and the second to be announced soon.

BHN brings together more than two decades of experience developing and producing the world's most prominent gatherings of the hotel and tourism investment community. At these events (more than 80 conferences completed or in development), more than 60,000 international delegates have come together to network, conduct business and learn about the latest trends.

This chapter connects you to our upcoming events and important players who are active in the investment equation -- lenders, brokers, developers, consultants, and others who contribute to the hospitality industry. Their network includes over 20,000 hotel industry leaders in 130 countries.

The Hotel Opportunities Latin America (HOLA) Conference is designed to provide an annual meeting place for hotel executives, investors, lenders, developers, and the professional advisory community who are interested in doing deals in one of the world's hottest hotel markets - Latin America.

HOLA will bring together the leaders in the hotel industry to discuss important trends, to network, to identify new opportunities, and to do deals through a combination of plenary sessions, breakout panels, and interactive development workshops. Program tracks on hotel investment in Mexico, Brazil, South America, and Central America will be featured.

If you are serious about the hotel business in Latin America, one can't afford to miss HOLA. HOLA will be held immediately after the Caribbean Hotel & Resort Investment Summit (CHRIS) at the JW Marriott Marquis Miami, Florida.

WHO SHOULD ATTEND

Investors, Owners, Lenders, Developers, Hotel Chain/ Management Company Executives, Investment Bankers, Vacation Ownership Executives, Financial Advisors, Real Estate & Financial Intermediaries, Builders, Consultants, Lawyers, Architects & Designers, Government Tourism Officials and Media

TWO HOTEL INVESTMENT CONFERENCES

The Tourism Business Council of South Africa (TBCSA) and UK-based Bench Events, who joined forces recently to extend the reach of the Hotel Investment Conference Africa (HICA) brand across the continent, will in 2011 host two conferences focusing on differing regions of Africa.

TBCSA are the originators of the HICA concept and Bench Events are well known for hosting premier conferences on hotel investment in Europe and the Middle East.

Chief Executive Officer of the TBCSA Mmatšatši Marobe says "Africa is a large and diverse continent of over 50 countries with many markets either emerging or evolving rapidly in central and northern regions, coupled with substantial and more mature markets in the southern areas.

"To reflect this and from continued demand, HICA - A focus on Southern Africa, will take place from 5 to 6 May, immediately before INDABA, Africa's largest tourism trade fair in Durban, and HICA - A focus on North and Central Africa, will take place in Casablanca from 26 to 27 September."

Grant Collier, Marketing Director of Bench Events says "There are many unique opportunities that both conferences wish to address. The southern event will focus on taking stock after the influx of visitors from the FIFA World Cup and will include a detailed look at the future investment climate in the south using actual case studies.

"In addition, the September event in Casablanca will focus on new opportunities emerging from changing political structures in the north and the developing markets of Central, West and East Africa.

"Like the southern event, the northern and central Africa conference is rapidly gaining much interest from both sponsors and delegates alike and it is anticipated that it too will become a 'must attend' event in the annual industry calendar."

About the Tourism Business Council of South Africa (TBCSA)

The Tourism Business Council of South Africa is the official umbrella organisation for the travel and tourism private sector in South Africa. As a corporate association, the TBCSA strives to work together with all role players to create an enabling environment for growth and development of the tourism industry. The TBCSA originated the HICA concept (www.hica.co.za) in 2007 and is the primary driver behind this annual industry event for Southern Africa.

The TBCSA) is made up of paying members from key travel and tourism associations, leading businesses as well as large corporations, who operate outside of the tourism sphere but recognise the overall value of tourism to the economy.

ABOUT BENCH EVENTS

Bench Events has a long track record in co-hosting the premier hotel investment events in Europe and the Middle East. Bench Events' Chairman, Jonathan Worsley, is one of the organisers and founders of the highly successful International Hotel Investment Forum now in its fourteenth year. In 2005, he was responsible for launching the Arabian Hotel Investment Conference in Dubai; in 2008 launched the Russia & CIS Hotel Investment Conference. In 2011 Bench Events co-hosts the Central Asia and Turkey Hotel Investment Conference, and will launch Hotel Investment Conference Africa, in Morocco.

Bench Events' sister company, JW Bench, is a benchmarking company that has successfully launched the Conference Bench and the Productivity Bench. An industry first, the Conference Bench measures performance data for conference and banqueting space in 10 cities throughout Europe and the Middle East.

CONDO HOTEL

A condo hotel, also known as a hotel-condo or a Condotel, is a building used as both a condominium and a hotel. Condo hotels are typically high-rise buildings developed and operated as luxury hotels, usually in major cities and resorts.These hotels have condominium units which allow someone to own a full-service vacation home. When they are not using this home, they can leverage the marketing and management done by the hotel chain to rent and manage the condo unit as it would any other hotel room.

The U.S. Government is very strict about the type of advertising that can be done vis-a-vis condo hotel projects. Some condo projects have advertised themselves as real estate investments, but since the value of these condos as a real estate investment is not entirely clear the U.S. Government currently disallows use of this reference when advertising condo hotels.

Condo hotels have been criticized in California for allowing developers to skirt laws designed to protect public access to beaches. Because such a facility has hotel rooms, it can be classified as a public accommodation, even though the majority of the units are privately held, and the facility does little to accommodate the public.

While not intended as a complete list, the most popular locations in the U.S. for condo hotels include: Aspen, Chicago, Miami, Fort Lauderdale, the Las Vegas metropolitan area, New York City, Myrtle Beach, South Carolina, and Orlando, Florida. Condo hotels are also found at ski resorts and international destinations, such as Jaco, Costa Rica. Investors spent an estimated $250 million on condo hotels in 2006, with much of that spending concentrated on resort areas.

COSTS

Note that analyzing the economics of a condo hotel unit is extremely difficult because of the challenge of getting accurate information about the potential income stream. Developers uniformly do not provide important data or estimates for room rates or occupancy levels for fear of coming under U.S. Securities and Exchange Commission (SEC) regulations on investments, as opposed to real estate regulations.

FINANCIAL CONSIDERATIONS

The primary factors that contribute to the financial outcome in ownership are rental revenue, appreciation or depreciation, lending and tax deductions. Rental revenue is shared with the management company, and owners typically pay no upfront fees for management, which includes the marketing and reservation of the units. Typical monthly fees for units in the rental pool include FF&E (Furniture, Fixtures and Equipment) reserve and resort fee(s).

Although the revenue splits between owner and management company do vary from project to project, most hover around 50 percent. Most condo hotels, and especially branded hotels like Westin or Ritz-Carlton, are strategically located in resort economies or popular urban destinations, which allow for high nightly rates and consistent year-round occupancy. Rental income from hotel guests is at the mercy of travel patterns and may decline.

Many condo hotels, especially the branded condo hotels, have seen double-digit growth, and have out-performed traditional condos or single family homes in the same resort market. Condo hotels units are fee simple deeded real estate, and can be bought and sold like other forms of real estate.

Because of the lack of resale data available for many of the emerging markets where pre-construction condo hotels can be found, experts heed caution when considering a condo hotel purchase for investment purposes alone. Just like traditional real estate, appreciation is never guaranteed. This very scenario most recently occurred in Las Vegas. Several of the more notable condo hotels have sold for less in the resale market than during pre-construction.

Financing is generally costlier than for a primary residence. Mortgage rates may be a full point higher, and in the past this was especially true because financial institutions were unfamiliar with the condo hotel concept. Pre-construction purchases require a significant down payment, and buyers will not see financial return or be able to use their unit until the hotel is completed and ready for operation. Furthermore owners may have to purchase extra insurance to protect against liability claims and some types of damage or loss.

Additional tax benefits may be obtained through condo hotel ownership. If the condo hotel is used for non-primary residence or residential rental, owners may be able to accelerate the depreciation on their condo hotel unit from 39 years, down to 27.5, 15, 7, and even 5 years. Condo hotel tax laws determine this, and affect individuals on a case-by-case basis, as each potential buyer's tax situation is different.

HOME-OWNER'S ASSOCIATION FEES AND SERVICES

As with most condominiums, owners of condo-hotel units are required to pay homeowner's association fees, commonly referred to as HOAs. The fee and services can vary a great deal. Factors causing a fluctuation are the hotel's star rating and operation level, and its physical location. A property located on the ocean, for example, can experience coastal weather regular basis, which in turn can increase the need for more regular maintenance to the exterior of the building. Along those same lines, a property located in a ski resort must weather powerful winter storms and must also deal with snow removal services.

Exceptions aside, many of the fees and services found in HOAs are fixed and fluctuate very little from project to project. Services such as these usually include general unit utilities, common area utilities, individual room and building reserves, grounds maintenance, exercise area use fees, security, pest control, mechanical repair costs, safety alarm systems, parking area maintenance, pool area maintenance, and owner management and administrative services. Items related to hotel guest impact are generally not included in the HOA fees, these would include housekeeping, and costs related to hotel staffing and operation.

HOTEL & MOTEL MANAGEMENT

Hotel and Motel Management magazine is a trade publication produced by Questex Media Group, Established in 1875, Hotel & Motel Management is a flagship trade publication that has been delivering hotel news, analysis and operational strategies for more than 134 years. Regular features include special reports, research/top lists, hot products, technology, furniture, fixtures and equipment, hotel operations and trends and statistics.

Hotel & Motel Management is also part of the HotelWorld Network, which provides access and opportunity within all facets of the hotel and lodging industry across the globe. It encompasses a series of publications and live events that serve the hospitality industry including Hotel & Motel Management magazine, Hotel Design magazine,which celebrates the design excellence of hotels, resorts, lodges and destination spas; Luxury Hotelier, a digital-only platform reaching the exclusive audience of four-and five-star hotel owners and operators; and The Hotel Times magazine, a digital-only platform focusing on international hotel investment and real estate.

In addition to these print and online products, the HotelWorld Network includes prominent events such as the International Hotel Investment Forum (IHIF) held in Berlin, which is the leading meeting place for the European hotel investment community; the Russia & CIS Hotel Investment Conference, which provides an invaluable opportunity to explore the region's enormous potential and uncover new business opportunities; HotelWorld Expo & Conference part of International Hospitality Week held in Las Vegas, which offers an international experience for hotel industry professionals and the industry's suppliers and manufacturers located throughout the world; the HOTEC series of three-day forums held across the globe which consist of pre-scheduled appointments with numerous networking opportunities to do business and exchange ideas with the leaders who influence the future of the global hospitality industry and introducing IHIF Asia Pacific , a newly-launched hotel investment conference in the Asia Pacific region.

While the impact of the devastating earthquake on Japanese investment is estimated to be short-lived, Japanese businesses will ultimately seek relocation to other countries including Thailand in an attempt to diversify risks.

Industry Minister Chaiwuti Bannawat said that the earthquake that hit Japan last week would prompt Japanese businesses to speed up expanding their investments in other countries in order to lower risks.

"Foreign direct investment is likely to drop in the short term but we will see an increase by the end of this year, due to relocation to Southeast Asia," said Mr Chaiwuti. Thanit Sorat, vice-chairman of the Federation of Thai Industries (FTI), said the earthquake would have both positive and negative effects on Thai exports.

On the positive side, it might cause Thai exports to expand, particularly by the food sector, as Japan buys more chicken and shrimp, as well as other canned foods to replenish inventories, said Mr Thanit.

Japan is among the biggest markets for Thai exports of poultry and shrimp.

On the negative side, businesses might face increased costs from having to find new markets to substitute some of the raw materials that have previously been imported from Japan.

"In the long term, Thailand will receive benefits because Japanese investors are saying that the concentration of industries in the same place is a risk, and therefore they will probably need to look for places to diversify their risks, including Thailand and Vietnam as their options," said Mr Thanit. Analysts said Thai oil companies should also benefit from rising refining margins and product spreads. Supply has been tight after several refiners in Japan had to close after Friday's earthquake

Pailin Chuchottaworn, president of IRPC, a chemical affiliate of PTT Plc, said prices of finished oil and petrochemical products are expected to rise after Japan's nuclear plants halted operations, affecting about 25% of the power supply in Japan

Viboon Kromadit, director and chief operating officer of Amata Corporation Plc, said Japan would recover at a fast rate since it has money, resources and technology. Investment will slow down in the short term since money will be needed for the recovery, but in the medium term, businesses will have to decide to relocate, he said. "Although they are already starting to do so, [the disaster] will make it easier for them to decide. And in this region, one of the safest places is Thailand, while the safest place in Thailand is the Eastern Seaboard," said Mr Viboon.

Sampan Silapanad, president of the Electronic and Computer Employers' Association, said electronics makers were working on backup plans in case it takes longer than expected for Japan to recover.

"There are a couple of Japanese parts suppliers for the hard disk drive (HDD) industry whose operations are affected by the quakes in terms of power supply and workforce," he said.

But these parts are not major components and HDD makers in Thailand have over a month's worth of inventory

"I think the current situation is manageable and will be resolved, possibly in one to two weeks. If it takes a month to recover, then there will be a problem," added Mr Sampan.

Somchai Sittichaisrichart, the managing director of SiS Distribution (Thailand), said there were signs that prices of flash memory used in digital devices and PC cards for notebook computers would increase shortly due to the closure of semiconductor factories in Japan.

Vira Intanate, chief executive of SVOA, said prices of flash memory would rise in the wake of the disaster as suppliers took advantage of the situation.

Atchaka Sibunruang, secretary general of the Board of Investment, said damages to Thailand's trade and investment had yet to be estimated but she noted that only products imported from Japan by Thailand would be affected.

Munenori Yamada, president and chief representative of the Japan External Trade Organisation (Jetro), said that despite the recent earthquake, Japan still offered potential investment opportunities to Thais in areas including research and development centres, business platforms and trendsetters, which include fashion and design.

INFORMATION TECHNOLOGY SHOWS

CeBIT

CeBIT is the world's largest and most international computer expo. CeBIT is held each year on the world's largest fairground in Hanover, Germany, and is a barometer of the state of the art in information technology. The trade fair is organized by Deutsche Messe AG.

With an exhibition area of roughly 450,000 m² (5 million ft²) and up to 850,000 visitors at the apex of the dot-com boom, it is larger both in area and attendance than its Asian counterpart COMPUTEX and the no-longer held American equivalent COMDEX. While by 2007 the CeBIT expo attendance had shrunk to around 200,000 from those all-time highs,, attendance rebounded to 334,000 by 2010. The 2008 expo was marred by the police raids of 51 exhibitors for patent infringement.

The 2011 expo was held from 1 to 5 March, 2011.

CeBIT was traditionally the computing part of the Hanover Fair, a big industry trade show held every year. It was first established in 1970, with the opening of the Hanover fairground's new Hall 1, then the largest exhibition hall in the world. However, in the 1980s the information technology and telecommunications part was straining the resources of the industry fair so much that it was given a separate trade show starting 1986, held four weeks earlier than the main Hanover Fair.

In 2009, the U.S. state of California became official Partner State of Germany's IT and telecommunications industry association, BITKOM, and of CeBIT 2009. focusing on environmentally-friendly technologies.

Other CeBIT-Branded Shows

As CeBIT continued to grow quickly and was becoming too big on its own, it was decided to concentrate on the professional market, while the home and entertainment market was given a separate show, CeBIT Home, during summer, planned to be biennial. However, after being held twice (in 1996 and 1998), the 2000 CeBIT Home (had originally been scheduled to be held in Leipzig due to the Expo 2000 being held in Hanover) was cancelled and the project was abandoned.

Since 1999 the CeBIT sponsor Deutsche Messe AG ("German Trade Show, Inc.") has organized trade shows outside of Germany bearing the CeBIT name:

- CeBIT Asia, in Shanghai, China
- CeBIT Australia, in Sydney
- CeBIT Eurasia Bili?im, in Istanbul, Turkey
- CeBIT America/USA in New York City, USA. It was held in 2003 and 2004, but subsequently cancelled in 2005.

CeBIT Global Conferences

Running over a five-day period in Hanover, Germany, the CeBIT Global Conferences (CGC) are staged congruently with the CeBIT exhibition. The conferences are dedicated to providing a 360° overview of the digital industry's four core markets: IT, Telecommunications, Digital Media and Consumer Electronics. Noted industry figures and researchers from across the globe are invited to speak on the latest relevant trends and innovations as well as their impact on society and the working world. The conference is divided up into keynote speeches, talks and panel discussions. The CGC conferences are produced by Deutsche Messe AG, with the German BITKOM association acting as the CGC patron since 2009.

Recent conferences have featured the following keynote themes:

- 2008: "Improving Life in the Global Village". This installment of CGC attracted 1900 visitors and 43 speakers attending the keynotes and discussion sessions.
- 2009: "How Will We Be Working, Living and Communicating in the Coming Years?" This CGC drew 3,133 visitors from 88 nations, with some 2,200 guests following the conference via live streaming.
- 2010: "The Challenges of a Changing World - ICT for Better Lives and Better Business", attracting some 4,000 guests from more than 100 nations. Just under 4,000 guests also visited the conference via live streaming.

The motto of the CeBIT Global Conferences for 2011 is "The Power of Creativity and Innovation". Speakers at the CeBIT Global Conferences have included Gov. Arnold Schwarzenegger, Governor of California; Kevin Turner, COO, Microsoft, Craig Barrett, Chairman of the Board, Intel, Jon Iwata SVP Marketing & Communications, IBM, Reid Hoffman, Chairman and CEO, LinkedIn; Scott Durchslag, COO, Skype; Dr. Werner Vogels, Vice President & CTO, Amazon, Stewart Butterfield, Co-founder of Flickr.com, Michael Jones, Chief Technology Advocate, Google & Founder of Google Earth; Mark Kingdon, CEO, LindenLab

CeBIT Awards

CeBIT has also become a platform for recognising achievement by ICT businesses, particularly in Australia. The awards include the Excellence in Communications Award, the Advanced Retail Technology Award, the Innovative IT

Security Award, and the Early Innovators Award. Notable past winners include Motorola, McAfee and eWAY.

BETT

BETT or The BETT show (formerly known as the British Educational Training and Technology Show) is an annual trade show in the United Kingdom that showcases the use of information technology in education. Founded in 1985, it has expanded to fill both the National and Grand Halls at the Olympia exhibition centre in London, England. BETT celebrated its 25th anniversary at the 2009 show.

The show was first held in January 1985 as the "Hi Technology and Computers in Education Exhibition" at the Barbican Centre, central London, in association with the British Educational Equipment Association. As the use of technology in education increased, so did the show, and had outgrown the Barbican by 1993, when the move to Olympia was made.

The show has also expanded from being a purely technology show, and whilst there are stands for companies ranging from multinationals Microsoft and Apple Inc. to small single-product firms, others attending include the Department for Children, Schools and Families, and teaching unions such as the NASUWT and National Union of Teachers.

A large number of seminars from well-known providers are held at BETT, which offer training (Continuing Professional Development) opportunities for education professionals.

Criticised in the past for perhaps marginalising teachers due to the increasing business nature of the show, the producers (EMAP) have introduced a number of teacher friendly events such as TeachMeet to tackle this.

Computer Security Conference

A computer security conference is a term that describes a convention for individuals involved in computer security. They generally serve as a meeting place for system and network administrators, hackers, and computer security experts. Common activities at hacker conventions may include:

- "Boot camps"- offering training and certification in Information Technology.
- Presentations from keynote speakers, or panels. Common topics include social engineering, lockpicking, penetration testing, and hacking tools.

General Computer Security Conferences

General security conferences are often held by security product vendor companies or organisations.

- ACSAC, Annual Computer Security Applications Conference
- ASIA or the Annual Symposium on Information Assurance that serves as the academic track for the New York State Cyber Security Conference , an annual information security conference held in Albany, NY usually for two days during June targeted at academic, government, and industry participants.
- AthCon, A yearly IT Security conference held in Greece.
- Black Hat, a series of conferences held annually in different cities around the world. Black Hat USA, held in Las Vegas immediately before DEF CON, is the largest 'official' computer security event in the world.
- BlueHat Conference, a twice a year, invitation-only Microsoft security conference aimed at bringing Microsoft security professionals and external security researchers together.
- CarolinaCon, in North Carolina, is a regional technology and network security conference usually held during Spring.
- ChicagoCon, Chicago's Ethical Hacking Conference.
- CONFidence, A yearly IT Security conference held in Europe.

- Department of Defense Cyber Crime Conference, an annual conference that focuses on the computer security needs of the United States federal government, military, and defense contractors.
- Hack.lu, an annual conference held in Luxembourg
- Hacker Halted, Presented by EC-Council, the objective of the global series of Hacker Halted conferences is to raise international awareness towards increased education and ethics in IT Security.
- Hack In Paris, Annual IT security conference held in Paris
- Hackito Ergo Sum, Security conference pertaining to research topics, with attendees and speakers from both the industry, the offensive side and the academic circles, held in Paris every April.
- RSA Security Conference, Cryptography and information security-related conference held annually in the San Francisco Bay Area.
- S4:SCADA Security Scientific Symposium, Security conference pertaining to SCADA held annually by Digital Bond, usually in Miami, FL.
- SANSFIRE, A yearly conference dedicated to the training of GIAC certified professionals, and networking with members of the SANS Internet Storm Center.
- SecureWorld Expo, A series of regional IT Security conferences offering education, CPE training opportunities, and networking of security leaders, experts, senior executives, and policy makers who shape the face of security.
- SOURCE Conference, SOURCE is a computer security conference in Boston, Seattle, and Barcelona that offers education in both the business and technical aspects of the security industry.
- TROOPERS IT Security Conference, Annual international IT Security event with workshops held in Heidelberg, Germany.

HACKER CONFERENCES

A hacker conference, also known as a hacker con, is a a convention for hackers. These serve as meeting places for phreakers, hackers, and security experts.

The actual events, timespans, and details of various themes of these conventions not only depends on the specific convention attended but also its perceived reputation. Typically the actual details of any given convention are couched in mild secrecy due to the legality of certain panels, as well as the willingness of attendees to explain themselves to law enforcement and less computer-savvy individuals (see hacker definition controversy).

Common topics include wardriving, lockpicking, corporate and network security, personal rights and freedoms, new technologies, as well as general 'geek' motifs. Some may also have contests and general collaborative events such as hackathons.

Annual Hacker Conventions

- BrumCon, yearly conference in Birmingham UK, held by Brum2600
- CanSecWest, large annual convention held in Vancouver, Canada.
- Chaos Communication Congress, the oldest and Europe's largest hacker conference, held by Chaos Computer Club.
- ClubHack, India's hacker convention.
- DEF CON, in Las Vegas, is the biggest hacker convention in the United States held during summer (June-August).
- C0c0n - Where Hack3rs Unite.
- Ekoparty, a hacker convention in Argentina and one of the most important in South America, held annually around September in Buenos Aires.
- HackCon - Norway's biggest security convention, held in Oslo, Norway.

- nullcon - Community driven Security and hacking conference (by null - The open security community).
- Hack In The Box, a security conference, Asia's largest network security conference held annually in Kuala Lumpur, Malaysia and more recently the Middle East.
- Hackers 2 Hackers Conference, a Brazilian conference.
- Hackfest, a Quebec, Canada, bilingual conferences and hacking games.
- Hackers on Planet Earth (H.O.P.E.), in New York is held by 2600: The Hacker Quarterly in mid-summer (July/August) every other year.
- Kiwicon, is a Wellington, New Zealand hacker convention.
- LayerOne, run every spring in Los Angeles, California.
- MalCon, world's first International Malware Conference, hosted in India.
- Notacon, in Cleveland, Ohio, is an art and technology conference held frequently in mid-April.
- Nuit du Hack, the first and oldest French annual hacker conference, held by HZV
- PhreakNIC, in Nashville, Tennessee, is held by Nashville 2600. around October.
- Pumpcon, in Philadelphia, Pennsylvania, is held around October.
- Pwn2Own, in Vancouver, Canada is held at the end of March, started 2007. Targets: web browsers and web related software.
- Quahogcon, In Providence, Rhode Island is held at the end of April.
- ROOTCON, in Cebu, Philippines is held around September-October. Philippines' premier hacker conference.
- Ruxcon, in Melbourne, Australia -- Ruxcon is the premier technical security conference in Australia. In

2010, Ruxcon will be held on Saturday November 20 and Sunday 21st Nov 2010.

- SEC-T, a hacking and security convention in Stockholm, Sweden.
- SecTor, a Toronto convention, founded in 2007 and seemingly held around October.
- ShakaCon, in Honolulu, Hawaii convention started in 2007 by Secure DNA held every spring.
- ShmooCon, a Washington DC convention started in 2005 by The Shmoo Group, and held annually in late winter (usually February).
- Summercon, one of the oldest hacker conventions, held during Summer (frequently in June). It helped set a precedent for more modern "cons" such as H.O.P.E. and DEF CON.
- THOTCON, a Chicago based hacker conference held in the Spring each year.
- ToorCon, San Diego hacker convention that emerged from the 2600 user group frequently in late September.
- Recon, A hacker convention primarily focused on Reverse Engineering. Held in or around July annually in Montréal, Québec.
- Nola X Con, a New Orleans based hacker conference that will debut in 2012.

Non-annual Hacker Conventions

Stichting HAL2001, a not-for-profit organization, holds a quadrennial Dutch hacker convention. They have, so far, held HAL2001 (Hackers at Large) and What the Hack (2005, originally called HEX (referring to the 16th anniversary of the event, as well as an acronym for Hacking Extreme)). The Dutch conferences held prior Stichting HAL2001's existence were Galactic Hacker Party (1989), Hacking at the End of the Universe (1993) and Hacking In Progress (1997), notable for being held simultaneously and in conjunction with Beyond

HOPE. The not-for-profit organization 'Stichting Hxx' is organizing the 2009 incarnation of this con; HAR. (Hacking at Random)

Hackers on Planet Earth

HOPE (abbreviation of Hackers on Planet Earth, in addition to being the first two letters in "Hotel Pennsylvania", the venue where the conference is held) is a conference series sponsored by the hacker magazine 2600: The Hacker Quarterly. There have been eight conferences to date.

HOPE: Hackers On Planet Earth

Held from August 13 to August 14, 1994, at the Hotel Pennsylvania, the first HOPE conference marked 2600: The Hacker Quarterly's 10th anniversary. Well over 1,000 people were in attendance, including speakers from around the world. Admission included access to a 28.8 kbit/s local network.

Beyond HOPE

From August 8 through August 10, 1997, Beyond HOPE moved the conference to the Puck Building. Attendance doubled, with 2000 attendees. Bell Technology Group helped to support the hackers. A TAP reunion and a live broadcast of Off the Hook took place (hear it here). Admission included a 10 Mbit/s local network.

H2K

In 2000, HOPE returned to the Hotel Pennsylvania, where all its successors would also be located. Between July 14 and July 16, 2000, the conference ran 24 hours a day, bringing in 2300 attendees. Jello Biafra gave a keynote speech. In this historic cultural exchange between the punk rock icon/free speech activist and the hacker community, Jello managed to draw powerful connections, despite not having any actual computer experience, and the EFF raised thousands of dollars. The conference admission included a working Ethernet and a T1 link to the internet.

H2K2

H2K2 (July 12-14, 2002) also ran 24 hours a day, this time with a theme of the United States of America homeland security Advisory System. H2K2 included two tracks of scheduled speakers, a third track reserved for last minute and self scheduled speakers, a movie room, Retrocomputing, musical performances, a State of the World Address by Jello Biafra, keynotes by Aaron McGruder and Siva Vaidhyanathan and discussions on the DMCA and DeCSS. Freedom Downtime premiered on Friday evening (July 14).

The conference admission included wireless 802.11b coverage and places to link in with wired Ethernet, an open computer area for access to a 24-hour direct uplink to the Internet at "T-1ish" speeds, a public cluster (pictures here) made available by The DataHaven Project, as well as an active internal network.

The Fifth HOPE

The Fifth H.O.P.E. (July 9-11, 2004) had a theme of propaganda and commemorated the anniversaries of both the H.O.P.E. cons and Off the Hook (with a live broadcast of the show from the con like at Beyond H.O.P.E.). Keynotes speakers were Kevin Mitnick, Steve Wozniak and Jello Biafra. There was also a media presentation by some of the "members" of the Phone Losers of America who celebrated their tenth-year anniversary. Additionally, Cult of the Dead Cow celebrated its twentieth anniversary at the conference. The conference admission included access to a four layer public network with two T1 lines + backup links to the internet via a Public Terminal Cluster, various wired means, a WiFi network on three floors and a video network.

HOPE Number Six

HOPE Number Six (July 21-23, 2006) included talks from Richard Stallman and Jello Biafra.Kevin Mitnick was scheduled to be at the conference but was unable to make it; while on vacation in Colombia an illness postponed his return.

Hope Number Six had a 100-megabit Internet connection, claimed by the organizers to be the fastest Internet connection at any US hacker conference. The event's theme was based around the series "The Prisoner" (as this event is titled "Number Six," a designation shared by the titular "prisoner,") and around the number 6 itself. Notable occurrences:

"Steve Rambam, a noted private investigator who runs Pallorium, Inc., an online investigative service, was set to lead a panel discussion titled "Privacy is Dead ... Get Over It." A few minutes before the start of the panel, Rambam was arrested by the FBI on charges that he unlawfully interfered with an ongoing case prosecutors filed against Albert Santoro, a former Brooklyn assistant district attorney who was indicted in Jan. 2003 with one count of money-laundering. The charges were eventually dropped and the talk was held in November 2006, long after the conference ended.

"Jello Biafra began his talk by referring to the above arrest, noting the convention had been more "spook heavy" than usual. He then announced a "special message" to "any Federal agents that may be in the audience", and mooned the convention.

The Last HOPE

The Last HOPE took place on July, 18-20, 2008 at the Hotel Pennsylvania. A notable change from past years was the use of an Internet forum to facilitate community participation in the planning of the event.

The name referred to the expectation that this would have been the final H.O.P.E. conference due to the scheduled demolition of its venue, the Hotel Pennsylvania. A 'Save The Hotel' campaign is ongoing, but it was revealed at the Closing Ceremony that the hotel's demolition plans were postponed indefinitely, and that The Next HOPE was scheduled for Summer 2010. It was at the closing ceremony that it was revealed that the use of the word "last" could also refer to the previous event, or one that had ended (referring to The Last HOPE itself).

Steven Levy gave the keynote address. Kevin Mitnick, Steve Rambam, Jello Biafra, and Adam Savage of MythBusters were also featured speakers. Descriptions and audio of the talks can be found at TheLastHOPE.org and their wiki.

The Next HOPE

The most recent HOPE convention, named "The Next HOPE", took place on July 16 - 18, 2010. The Next HOPE was held at the Hotel Pennsylvania, as the plans by Vornado to demolish the hotel are on hold.

SHMOOCON

ShmooCon is an American hacker convention organized by The Shmoo Group. There are typically about 35 different talks and presentations, on a variety of subjects related to computer security and cyberculture.

From 2005 to 2010, ShmooCon was held at the Wardman Park Marriott Hotel in Washington, D.C.. ShmooCon 2011 was held at the Washington Hilton, in Washington, D.C..

- February 4-6, 2005: approximately 400 attendees
- January 13-15, 2006: approximately 700 attendees
- March 23-25, 2007: Sold out; over 900 attendees
- February 15-17, 2008: Sold out; over 1200 attendees
- February 6-8, 2009: Sold out; over 1600 attendees
- February 5-7, 2010: Sold out; around 1600 attendees
- January 28-30, 2011: Sold out; over 1600 attendees

Research Presented at ShmooCon

ShmooCon seeks to select talks that are original research, and have not been presented yet at other conventions.

Charitable Efforts

In 2011, ShmooCon t-shirt sales went 100% to support a charity of the purchasers choice. ShmooCon reports that the final totals were $5010 for the EFF and $7640 for Hackers For Charity.

TOORCON

ToorCon is San Diego's exclusive hacker conference that traditionally takes place in late September. Started originally by the San Diego 2600 user group, ToorCon was founded in 1999 by Ben Greenberg and David Hulton (h1kari). The first year it was held at the University of California, San Diego's Price Center and was later moved to the San Diego Concourse for the 2nd and 3rd year.

The 4th year was held at the Westin, 5th and 6th at the Manchester Grand Hyatt, and most recently the 7th to 10th conferences were held at the San Diego Convention Center. Starting in 2007, ToorCon Seattle was held at Last Supper Club, Pioneer Square, Seattle, Washington. ToorCon attracts many of the top leaders in the computer security community and has been known for its small-conference atmosphere, bringing together around 400 attendees annually.

Talks at ToorCon range from device hacking and reverse engineering, to protocol analysis, cryptographic algorithms, and all-around security issues. Each year ToorCon has a particular theme to the talks, and is split into two opposing tracks. In 2006, the theme was "Bits and Bytes." in 2005, the theme was "Smoke and Mirrors."

Along with two parallel tracks that run over the course of ToorCon weekend, there are also vendor tables and games. Usually featuring at least one book publisher such as Syngress or No Starch Press, a hardware vendor, and a t-shirt printer. Capture the Flag is one of the recurring games over the weekend.

11

HOSPITALITY INDUSTRY TRADE SHOWS

The hospitality industry consists of broad category of fields within the service industry that includes lodging, restaurants, event planning, theme parks, transportation, cruise line, and additional fields within the tourism industry. The hospitality industry is a several billion dollar industry that mostly depends on the availability of leisure time and disposable income. A hospitality unit such as a restaurant, hotel, or even an amusement park consists of multiple groups such as facility maintenance, direct operations (servers, housekeepers, porters, kitchen workers, bartenders, etc.), management, marketing, and human resources.

A trade fair is an exhibition organized so that companies in a specific industry can showcase and demonstrate their latest products, service, study activities of rivals and examine recent market trends and opportunities. In contrast to consumer fairs, only some trade fairs are open to the public, while others can only be attended by company representatives (members of the trade, e.g. professionals) and members of the press, therefore trade shows are classified as either "Public" or "Trade Only".

A few fairs are hybrids of the two; one example is the Frankfurt Book Fair, which is trade-only for its first three days and open to the general public on its final two days. They are held on a continuing basis in virtually all markets and normally attract companies from around the globe. For example, in the

U.S. there are currently over 2500 trade shows held every year, and several online directories have been established to help organizers, attendees, and marketers identify appropriate events.

The hospitality industry covers a wide range of organizations offering food service and accommodation. The hospitality industry is divided into sectors according to the skill-sets required for the work involved. Sectors include accommodation, food and beverage, meeting and events, gaming, entertainment and recreation, tourism services, and visitor information.

Modern trade fairs follow in the tradition of trade fairs established in late medieval Europe, in the era of merchant capitalism. In this era, produce and craft producers visited towns for trading fairs, to sell and showcase products.

Trade fairs often involve a considerable marketing investment by participating companies. Costs include space rental, design and construction of trade show displays, telecommunications and networking, travel, accommodations, and promotional literature and items to give to attendees. In addition, costs are incurred at the show for services such as electrical, booth cleaning, internet services, and drayage (also known as material handling). Consequently, cities often promote trade shows as a means of economic development.

Exhibitors attending the event are required to use an exhibitor manual or online exhibitor manual to order their required services and complete any necessary paperwork such as health and safety declarations. An increasing number of trade fairs are happening online, and these events are called virtual tradeshows. They are increasing in popularity due to their relatively low cost and because there is no need to travel whether you are attending or exhibiting.

COMPETITION & USAGE RATE

Usage rate is an important variable for the hospitality industry. Just as a factory owner would wish to have his or her productive asset in use as much as possible (as opposed to having to pay fixed costs while the factory isn't producing), so do restaurants, hotels, and theme parks seek to maximize the number of customers they "process" in all sectors. This led to formation of services with the aim to increase usage rate provided by hotel consolidators. Information about required or offered products are brokered on business networks used by vendors as well as purchasers.

In viewing various industries, "barriers to entry" by newcomers and competitive advantages between current players are very important. Among other things, hospitality industry players find advantage in old classics (location), initial and ongoing investment support (reflected in the material upkeep of facilities and the luxuries located therein), and particular themes adopted by the marketing arm of the organization in question (such as a restaurant called the 51st fighter group that has a World War II theme in music and other environmental aspects). Very important is also the characteristics of the personnel working in direct contact with the customers. The authenticity, professionalism, and actual concern for the happiness and well-being of the customers that is communicated by successful organizations is a clear competitive advantage.

Hospitality Industry becomes the center of business activity for hotel business and hospitality industry which gives potential and current market players of hotels construction and hotel arrangements branch an opportunity to familiarize with a complex of offers on establishment of hotels with a turn-key solution.

Visitor's Profile

The target audience of the forum are distinctly selected customers, industry specialists and owners of hotels, manufactures and suppliers of equipment, goods and services, managers of operating hotels in Russia and abroad, organizations and businessmen planning to open new hotels and thus carrying out reconstruction and modernization of the branch, regional representatives of hotel business.

Exhibitor's Profile

Profile for exhibit include Front-of-house & Back-of-house systems, Tableware, Room Service, Signage, Restaurant Equipment, Food Manufacturing or Foodstuffs, Spa & Leisure Equipment, Kitchen Appliances, Hotel Furniture, Food Preparation Equipment, IT Services.

Event Name	:	The Hotel Show 2011
Date	:	17th - 19th May 2011
Venue	:	Dubai World Trade Centre (DWTC)
City/State	:	Dubai
Country	:	United Arab Emirates

Event Profile

The Hotel Show 2011 will take place at the Dubai World Trade Centre from 17th - 19th May 2011 for its 12th edition. The show is renowned for its world class display of products, designs and technologies and will showcase the full spectrum of the hospitality industry. In 2010, The Hotel Show welcomed 365 exhibitors from 35 countries and attracted 10,277 key industry decision makers from 78 countries worldwide. Join The Hotel Show 2011 and access a market valued at over US $30bn with an ongoing projects pipeline of over 450 hotels and 1,500 F&B outlets across the GCC, Middle East & Levant markets.

Highlights

- Exclusive trade fair for the hospitality industry in the MENA and GCC region
- Over 10,000 buyers from 78 countries attended the show last year
- Access a Hospitality market valued at over US $30bn 4.Global Conferences & Seminars dealing with current issues in the industry
- Visit The Corporate Catwalk showcasing uniforms for hospitality industry

- Live Demonstrations of products
- Networking functions and industry association meetings

VIRTUAL TRADESHOW

A virtual tradeshow (sometimes called a virtual trade air) is a type of virtual event run in an online environment, which goes live and stays live online for a limited period of time. It can be considered the online equivalent of a traditional tradeshow or exhibition, but exhibitors and visitors connect with one another via the Internet, regardless of geographic location, to exchange valuable information.

The "virtual tradeshow" was first publicly described and presented as "ConventionView" by Alan Saperstein and Randy Selman of Visual Data Corporation now know as Onstream Mediain April 1993 in a presentation to investors at the Waldorf Astoria hotel in New York city. The company was videotaping trade show exhibitors booths and then attaching the videos to HTML floor maps. Although Conventionview met with some early success the company closed it down returning to the market with a multimedia virtual tradeshow platform called MarketPlace365 in November 2010.

Typical Structure

The structure of a typical virtual tradeshow often includes a virtual exhibition hall which users enter with specific permissions and capabilities. Exhibitors can build virtual stands or booths to exhibit information related to their products or services, just as they would at a trade fair in a convention center; visitors view these virtual trade show displays in the exhibition hall. Users - both exhibitors and visitors - within the environment often create avatars as a visual representation of themselves.

Like their physical counterparts, virtual tradeshows may have other components such as a web conference, a web seminar ('webinar'), or other educational presentations. The virtual trade fair thus provides live interaction between users on several levels (one-to-one, one-to-few, one-to-many and many-to-many) and simultaneously.

Detailed tracking mechanisms allow organisers to determine the flow of traffic in the virtual tradeshow. Although virtual tradeshows are usually conducted in specialised web environments, some have been organised and conducted in tightly controlled text-based environments.

Virtual tradeshows can be used for international tradeshows, business match-makers, procurement fairs, or product launches. The experience also translates well for other applications such as virtual job fairs, virtual benefits fairs, online employee networks, distributor fairs, and venture capital fairs.

Providers of virtual event platforms have seen immense growth in the demand for their products partly attributable to the 2009-2010 recession driving cost-cutting approaches to business.

According to a Champion Exposition Services study, one in four people planned to use a digital event platform in the association market. The study also found that 70% of "respondents are actively producing, considering or interested in pursuing virtual events." However, many were not looking to replace physical events, but add on virtual components.

Visitor Facilities

Visitors to a virtual tradeshow usually fill out an online registration form to create an online badge, and then enter a virtual exhibit hall to visit virtual booths. The virtual booths often reflect the imagery of a real-world tradeshow booth with desks and displays (this similarity helps users relate to them more easily).

A virtual booth typically has several icons which can trigger different responses upon the click of the mouse. For example, visitors might initiate instant communication with the exhibitor via an instant message, email or a voice-call. Icons might also deliver multimedia such as videos and audio messages or other slide-show presentations.

Exhibitor Facilities

Virtual exhibitors use online tools to upload relevant and tailored content to appeal to the audiences. Virtual exhibits may be made to look like an exhibitor's real-world booth in any in-person trade fair where they may be exhibiting.

While some events are online-only, virtual tradeshows could also be run in conjunction with real-world or in-person tradeshows, creating 'hybrid events'. Virtual tradeshows typically cost much less than traditional trade shows.

Since virtual trade shows can be conducted from a person's desk, the cost of travel, lodging and physical construction of a trade show display is eliminated (exhibitors will usually, of course, be charged for the privilege of having an online stand at the virtual tradeshow).

Everyone can earn extra money online through trading. Forex is one of the best ways to earn quick cash. You just have to know the basic skills of trading, and you will be on your way to making money at home. You don't have to sit around your computer waiting after placing your trade. Just place your trade and wait for the profits to roll in in that way you will earn money.

Get as much information about forex before considering trading. Forex means means foreign exchange. That means buying a currency and selling it to make profit. Get familiar with forex terms used in forex trading. There are e-books online, with lots of information to get you started. Choose a forex broker or you can trade by yourself.

Decide which pair of currency will earn you the most money. Not all the time you will earn on the trades so just prepare on the losses. Expect to encounter risks of losing some of your investment capital, for the opportunity to make higher returns.

FRANKFURT TRADE FAIR

Frankfurt Trade Fair with 450,000,000 Euros in sales (preliminary figures 2010) and over 1,700 employees, is one of the world's largest trade fair companies. The group has a global network of 28 subsidiaries, five branch offices, and 52 international sales partners. Thus, the Messe Frankfurt is present in over 150 countries to their customers. At more than 30 locations in the world events "made by Messe frankfurt" take place. In 2010, Messe Frankfurt organised a total of 88 trade fairs, of which more than half took place outside Germany. At 578,000 square metres, Messe Frankfurt currently has nine exhibition halls, a central logistics centre, and an attached convention centre. The company is in the public sector, the shareholders are the City of Frankfurt, with 60 percent and the State of Hesse with 40 percent. The Board of Management of Messe Frankfurt consists of Wolfgang Marzin, Detlef Braun, and Uwe Behm.

Frankfurt is the third-largest trade fair in the world. It has a total area of 578,000 square metres (6,221,540 square feet). It has nine halls with a total of 321,754 square meters (3,463,331 square feet) of exhibition space and 96,078 square metres (1,034,175 square feet) of outdoor area more available.

The exhibition grounds is located in the Bockenheim and Westend-South districts in the west of Frankfurt. It has direct highway access (the Bundesautobahn 648) and parking on the Vine Area. By public transport it on the subway - and tram station Festhalle / Messe (lines U4, 16 and 17) and the S-Bahn station Messe Frankfurt (lines S3 to S6) to reach.

Architecture

The oldest building in the Trade Fair grounds is the Festhalle, a self-supporting dome structure made of steel and glass that was first opened to visitors on 19 May 1909.In the 1980s, the fairgrounds was enlarged into its present form. A tall Hammering Man sculpture stands on the pavement near its main entrance.

NAMM SHOW

The NAMM Show is one of the largest music product trade shows in the world, founded in 1901. It is held every

January in Anaheim, California, USA, at the Anaheim Convention Center. Its only major competitor is the Musik Messe in Frankfurt.

NAMM is a trade-only business show catering to domestic and international dealers and distributors, and the product exhibits are an integral part of the show, allowing the dealers and distributors to see what's new, negotiate deals and plan their purchasing for the next 6 to 12 months.

Only employees of the exhibiting manufacturers and/or NAMM member retailers and distributors are allowed to attend, along with credentialed members of the press. Exhibitors are allotted a specific number of badges based on the square footage of their booth, after which a $25 fee per badge is assessed. Dealers are allowed a certain number of badges based on different criteria.

The acronym NAMM originally stood for the National Association of Music Merchants, but has evolved from a national entity representing the interests of music products retailers to an international association including commercial, reseller members, affiliates and manufacturers.

The association's other show, Summer NAMM, takes place in July in Nashville, TN, at the downtown Nashville Convention Center. The smaller Summer NAMM is approximately one quarter the size of the NAMM Show in January and focuses more on industry meetings and professional development courses than products.

Recent reports indicated that the Summer NAMM show has suffered from declining attendance, as it has been cycled between Nashville, TN, Austin, TX and Indianapolis, IN during successive years.

WORLD POKER TOUR

The World Poker Tour (WPT) is a series of international poker tournaments featuring most of the world's professional players. It was started in the United States by attorney/ television producer Steven Lipscomb, who served as CEO of

WPT Enterprises (WPTE), the firm that controlled the World Poker Tour up to November 2009.

In 2008, the WPT started offering bracelets to its event champions. Players who won a title prior to the release of the WPT Bracelet, were given one retroactively. In November 2009, PartyGaming announced its acquisition of the World Poker Tour from WPTE for $12,300,000.

The World Poker Tour is a collection of Texas hold 'em poker tournaments held internationally, but mainly in the United States. The television show and the broadcasts of the World Series of Poker have led to a boom in the table game across American homes, in local casino poker rooms and online. The key sponsors of the tour are casinos and online poker sites. The show, which is syndicated internationally, is co-hosted by World Series of Poker bracelet winner Mike Sexton, and actor Vince Van Patten. Shana Hiatt served as the show host and sideline reporter in its first three seasons. Courtney Friel took over the host role for the fourth season, and Sabina Gadecki for the fifth. Layla Kayleigh and Kimberly Lansing began serving as hostesses in season six. Poker player and reporter Amanda Leatherman was the hostess for season seven. For Season 9 (2011), the show is being aired on Fox Sports Net with Kimberly Lansing returning as the host.

The tour had its debut season in the latter part of 2002 and early part of 2003, climaxing with the WPT Championship in April 2003 at the Bellagio in Las Vegas, Nevada. The first season aired on the Travel Channel on American cable television in the spring of 2003. The show made its network debut on February 1, 2004 on NBC with a special "Battle Of Champions" tournament, which aired against CBS coverage of the Super Bowl XXXVIII pre-game show. The Travel Channel aired the first five seasons of the Tour.

In April 2007, WPTE announced that the series would move to GSN for its sixth season in the spring of 2008. The first WPT tournament to air on GSN, the Mirage Poker Showdown, debuted on March 24, 2008. In July 2008, WPTE announced that the series would move to Fox Sports Net for its seventh season. The drawing power of the WPT, and most other poker tournaments, is that anyone who can pay the "buy-in" (an amount ranging from $2,500 to $25,000) or win a "satellite" tournament is able to compete against the top professional players.

In 2004, the World Poker Tour created a Walk of Fame, inducting poker legends Doyle Brunson and Gus Hansen, as well as actor James Garner.

The first three seasons of WPT are available on NTSC DVD. A series of spin-off tournaments, titled the Professional Poker Tour, began filming in 2004. Broadcast of the series was delayed, which was partly due to a dispute with the Travel Channel over rights. In the fall of 2005, WPTE announced that "a cable channel" (believed to be ESPN) had withdrawn from bidding for the PPT series, and that WPTE was negotiating with the Travel Channel to air the series.

On January 30, 2006, WPTE and the Travel Channel announced that they had dismissed all open lawsuits. The series began regular broadcast July 5, 2006, but was suspended after one season as WPTE couldn't find a television home for a second season.

An interesting side note is that only 4 players have finshed in the money at least once in all 8 seasons of the World Poker Tour. These players are Phil Hellmuth, Erik Seidel, Mark Seif, and Surinder Sunar.

The WPT has become a truly recognizable brand in poker and many believe they were one of the primary sparks to ignite the poker boom in the United States. The strength of the WPT brand can be seen in many products related and unrelated to poker i.e. playing cards, poker chips and tables, coffee mugs, clothing, key chains, notepads, watches, etc.

●●●

BIBLIOGRAPHY

Jacques Derrida (2000). *Of Hospitality*. Trans. Rachel Bowlby. Stanford: Stanford University Press.

Steve Reece (1993). *The Stranger's Welcome: Oral Theory and the Aesthetics of the Homeric Hospitality Scene*. Ann Arbor: The University of Michigan Press.

Mireille Rosello (2001). Postcolonial Hospitality. The Immigrant as Guest. Standford, CA: Stanford University Press.

Newth, A.M. (1967). *Britain and the World: 1789-1901*. New York: Penguin Books. p. 97. ISBN 0140803041.

Syed Ali. *Dubai: Gilded Cage* (Yale University Press; 2010) 240 pages. Focuses on the Arab emirate's treatment of foreign workers.

Heiko Schmid: *Economy of Fascination: Dubai and Las Vegas as Themed Urban Landscapes*, Berlin, Stuttgart 2009, ISBN 978-3-443-37014-5

Michael Corkery Condo Hotels: The Latest Twist In Buying a Vacation Residence The Wall Street Journal Online February 28, 2006

Millions bathe at Hindu festival *BBC News*, January 3, 2007.

Von Drehle, David (2007-07-23). Photographs by Greg Miller. "A new Day at the Fair". *Time* **170** (4): 50. ISSN 0040-781X.

- "Carneytown - Planning - Ride Company and Vendors". Retrieved 2007-08-27.
- "North American Midway Entertainment Event Schedule 2007". Archived from the original on 2007-07-26.
- Von Drehle, David (2007-07-23). Photographs by Greg Miller. "A new Day at the Fair". *Time* **170** (4): 50. ISSN 0040-781X.
- McClure, James (2008-06-12). "A Primer: The 'First Capital' Debate". YDR.com. http://www.ydr.com/ci_9569289. Retrieved 2010-07-26.
- Wilson, Kenneth G. (1993). *The Columbia Guide to Standard American English*. New York: Columbia University Press, pp. 27–28. ISBN 0-231-06989-8.
- Zimmer, Benjamin (2005-11-24). "Life in These, Uh, This United States". University of Pennsylvania—Language Log. Retrieved 2008-02-22.
- Lubowski, Ruben, Marlow Vesterby, and Shawn Bucholtz (2006-07-21). "AREI Chapter 1.1: Land Use". Economic Research Service.Retrieved 2009-03-09.
- Peter Weidhaas, Wendy A. Wright: *A History of the Frankfurt Book Fair*. Dundurn, October 31, 2007, ISBN 978-1550027440

INDEX